THE ECONOMIC BACKGROUND
TO AGRICULTURAL POLICY

THE
ECONOMIC BACKGROUND
TO
AGRICULTURAL POLICY

BY

EDITH H. WHETHAM, M.A.

*Gilbey Lecturer in the History and Economics of Agriculture
in the University of Cambridge
Fellow of Newnham College*

CAMBRIDGE
THE UNIVERSITY PRESS
1960

CAMBRIDGE UNIVERSITY PRESS
Cambridge, New York, Melbourne, Madrid, Cape Town,
Singapore, São Paulo, Delhi, Mexico City

Cambridge University Press
The Edinburgh Building, Cambridge CB2 8RU, UK

Published in the United States of America by Cambridge University Press, New York

www.cambridge.org
Information on this title: www.cambridge.org/9781107622111

© Cambridge University Press 1960

First published 1960
First paperback edition 2013

A catalogue record for this publication is available from the British Library

ISBN 978-1-107-62211-1 Paperback

FOR MY FATHER

WILLIAM CECIL DAMPIER

(formerly Whetham)

1867–1952

PREFACE

I have tried in this book to provide an analysis of agricultural policies in a form suitable for students of agriculture, for practitioners in farming and for other persons interested in agricultural planning. The more important factors influencing agricultural policies are described against a background of changing techniques of production and of changing demands from the buyers of agricultural products. I have concentrated mainly on the recent history of the United Kingdom but I have also drawn illustrations from other countries, in order to show the operation of agricultural policies, and of economic forces, in differing contexts.

EDITH H. WHETHAM

School of Agriculture,
Cambridge

CONTENTS

ix

CONTENTS

LIST OF TABLES

CONTENTS

LIST OF FIGURES

ABBREVIATIONS

E.J.   Economic Journal
F.A.O.   Food and Agriculture Organisation of the United Nations
I.C.A.E.   International Conference of Agricultural Economists
J.A.E.   Journal of Agricultural Economics
J.R.A.S.   Journal of the Royal Agricultural Society.
J.R.S.S.   Journal of the Royal Statistical Society
R.I.I.A.   Royal Institute for International Affairs
O.E.E.C.   Organisation for European Economic Co-operation

CHAPTER I

THE OBJECTIVES OF AGRICULTURAL POLICY

I. AGRICULTURAL OBJECTIVES

The title of this chapter assumes the existence of political entities called nations, each equipped with an effective Government and an agricultural policy. A decision to have no agricultural policy—to leave the development of farming to the play of market forces—is of course a major decision of policy; it was the policy effective in the United Kingdom during the ninety years from the repeal of the Corn Laws to the agricultural depression of the nineteen-thirties. But in the twentieth century, and especially since two world wars disrupted international markets, Governments have favoured more active policies for agriculture; they have encouraged, regulated, subsidised and stimulated various types of farming, for a variety of reasons and by a variety of methods. Agricultural economists can no longer assume that an active Government policy is an exception to the normal rule of a freely operating market; the study of agricultural economics, even in its elementary stages, must start from the assumption that Governments have agricultural policies, and sufficiently developed administrations to make their decisions reasonably effective.

It has become common for Governments to fashion plans for the development of their national economies; such plans vary in effectiveness from a pious wish publicised by some Minister of State to detailed control of individual industries and firms, as in eastern Europe. The objective of full employment, for instance, necessarily involves the existence, either in fact or in reserve, of fairly comprehensive powers over national finance and capital investment, in which agriculture must also be involved. Even this minimum of economic planning must therefore include some general concept of the desired role of agriculture; while in many countries the security of food supplies is of crucial importance, and in others the export of agricultural produce dominates foreign trade and the internal price structure. To separate out for study the planning of agriculture creates a somewhat artificial distinction in the field of economic policy; the justification for this course lies partly in the peculiarities of agriculture and partly in the interest which we all take in food.

During and after the second world war, agricultural planning became a highly complex matter in most countries. The administrative improvisations developed in the years of depression were extended into food rationing and price control in varying degrees. Since the end of the war many countries have been involved in acute problems over their balance of payments; and agricultural policies have reflected these post-war strains as well as the wider aspirations of social policy and national welfare. There is therefore no lack of material for any analysis of the economic basis of agricultural planning. But since each country has its own peculiarities in farming technique and economic structure, I propose to draw examples mainly from the United Kingdom, from New Zealand, and from the United States; the first being an importer of food, the second being an exporter of food, and the third having a wealth of statistics which illuminate its economic growth.

The activities of mankind do not lend themselves to logical classification in well-defined categories. Especially in the political world, legislation promoted for one reason may be continued for others and may develop quite unplanned results in the process of administration. But some classification of agricultural policies, however imprecise, is a necessary preliminary to a reasoned discussion of them. Let us start with four main groups, into one of which most intentions can be squeezed.

1. Maximisation of the national output .. .. .. (Plenty)
2. Maintenance of food supplies .. .. (Strategy)
3. Reducing variability in agricultural incomes .. .. (Stability)
4. Redistribution of personal incomes .. .. .. (Equality)

Let us look briefly at examples of each, bearing in mind that measures appropriate to achieve a certain policy in one country may have no relevance to the problems of a second which is at a different stage of development.

I. PLENTY

A country which aims at plenty attempts to secure the maximum increase in the supply of goods and services. In the modern world, the concept implies not a rise from one static level to another but a constant and continuing rise in the 'standard of living' for the majority of the people. For this policy, two points can be said to have fairly general relevance.

A continuing increase in the output of goods and services implies an inevitable conflict between present and future; immediate consumption may have to be cut if resources are to be made available for building a dam which will supply in the future both more irrigated land and more electric power for industry. And the poorer the country, the more urgent is the maintenance of immediate consumption and the more difficult it is to find resources to devote to capital equipment for the future. Conflict is also inevitable between the natural forces of custom and inertia, and the mobility of manpower over space and between occupations which is involved in rapid economic growth.

Secondly, a country which is open to foreign trade has greater opportunities for increasing its wealth than one which has to raise itself by its own bootstraps, using only its local resources. By borrowing from elsewhere, a country can improve its capital resources without an appreciable loss of current consumption; repayment can be effected out of the rising output to be expected when railways have been built, export crops established and local industries developed. Further, specialisation between countries enables a given output to be achieved with fewer resources, thus enabling all to be richer. In the last quarter of the nineteenth century, for instance, Britain specialised in the production of railway material which was used in America, Canada and Australia to open up the new lands from which grain was sent back to Britain; the price of bread fell markedly in Britain with a consequent improvement

3

in the general standard of consumption, although there was financial distress among those farmers and landowners whose income was derived from cereal crops. A similar trend is seen in New Zealand which grew most of its own wheat supply in the nineteenth century. But in the last thirty years a greater total output of goods and services has been obtained by importing much of the extra wheat required from Australia, by devoting the land and labour to the production of fat lambs and dairy produce, by selling these in Britain, and by using part of the proceeds to pay for the Australian wheat, and the remainder to import British china and American oil. Compared with both Britain and Australia, New Zealand has in its climate and pastures a 'comparative advantage' for the output of meat and dairy produce, and Australia for wheat production. Such specialisation between countries obviously involves certain risks, both of the physical interruption to transport and of the breakdown of the delicate mechanism of international payments; the achievement of plenty, therefore, may perhaps conflict with strategy.

2. STRATEGY

A country which has to import part of its food consumption has to consider the security of its supply. Supply may be liable to interruption because the exporting country ceases to export, because transport is stopped by war, or because the importing country lacks the means to pay on the international market. Drawing supplies from a large number of friendly countries is obviously the best security, but if this is not feasible, Governments may adopt a wide variety of measures to encourage the production at home of a greater supply of essential foodstuffs, even though this implies going without other commodities which could have been produced with the same resources.

3. STABILITY

There are three main causes of the instability of agricultural incomes over time. There is the short, but often violent, fluctuations caused by variations in crop yields from one year to another. Secondly, there are the more general fluctuations created primarily by fluctuations in aggregate demand associated with the trade cycle. Thirdly, a particular class of agricultural incomes may diverge from the general trend because the conditions of supply or of demand are undergoing a permanent change to which the economic structure is not yet fully adapted.

It is only quite recently that fluctuations in income have come to be regarded as undesirable, as something to be prevented or at least mitigated; the two great price falls of the inter-war years—from 1920 to 1922 and from 1929 to 1933—which affected almost all countries in varying degrees, left an indelible mark on the evolution of economic policies. The prevention of the second type of fluctuation—the maintenance of full employment, as it has come to be styled—is a recognised objective of Governments, most of which now possess wide powers to regulate investment, foreign exchanges and the money markets. These general powers aimed at the prevention of the most general type of fluctuation have been reinforced by a mass of purely agricultural legislation, inherited largely from the years of depression, but which can also be used to mitigate the fluctuations in agricultural incomes arising from the other causes.

4. EQUALITY

In a society based on private enterprise and the free choice of employment, the desirable distribution of capital and of labour between employments can only be secured by the offer of different incomes to the owners of these resources. The resulting inequalities in income have at times been found undesirable from other points of view; a great disparity in wealth is in itself sometimes regarded as an evil, which, unless corrected, is apt to increase by inheritance and aggregation. Most Governments now undertake a considerable redistribution of income and sometimes of capital by a variety of measures which affect agriculture as well as other industries. Taxes on income, taxes on inheritance, compulsory insurance against sickness and old age are obvious examples, but other measures operate through the mechanism of prices and markets. The suppression of monopolies or, on the other hand, the encouragement of monopolies may alter prices and therefore the distribution of incomes between groups of citizens, as may the control of rents and the enforcement of minimum wages. Many countries have imposed a maximum size of holding so as to prevent a small number of persons from aggregating land while others must work as landless labourers without security or status.

II. THE ROLE OF PRICES IN A MARKET ECONOMY

By choosing the agricultural policies of industrial countries for analysis we assume a commercial agriculture, working for non-agricultural markets and not primarily for the food supply of its operators. Farmers in such countries are mostly business men, seeking the greatest monetary return, though other motives also influence their actions. In making the most of their opportunities, they work through a system of prices— prices for the goods and services they buy, prices for the goods they sell. Agricultural planning also works mainly through the pricing system, raising some prices and lowering others, restricting the opportunities of some people to operate at certain prices while encouraging others. Observed from a central Planning Office, prices provide a method of inducing individuals to perform certain functions, and to offer the use of property which they control. On the assumption that most citizens are seeking most of the time to secure for themselves the greatest real income, a system of prices thus encourages individuals to produce voluntarily the huge variety of goods required in a complex industrial society. If more milk is required and less bacon, then a higher price for milk and a lower price for pigs will induce farmers to devote more resources of land, labour, capital and management to the upkeep of dairy cows and less to the upkeep of pigs. Higher profits to dairy farmers will enable them to outbid the pig-keepers in wages for men and rents for land; higher wages for dairymen will encourage some pig-keepers to master the intricacies of a milking machine.

Changes in prices thus become translated into changes in

incomes for the individuals who offer certain services as land-owners, farmers and pig-keepers. To a certain extent, prices will distribute incomes in proportion to the efficiency of individuals within each trade; an efficient dairy farmer will usually obtain a higher income than the inefficient, from the same system of prices. To a certain extent, again, prices will distribute incomes in proportion to the efficiency of individuals in offering the services most urgently required by consumers at any particular moment; the pigman who becomes a cowman when milk prices are rising will usually earn a larger income than the man who continues to produce pigs on a falling market. The employment of resources in the required amounts depends on inequalities of income; if all incomes were com-pulsorily equalised, the appropriate distribution of land, capital, and manpower could presumably be secured only by the wholesale compulsion on persons and their property.

At the other end of the market, the spending of incomes by individuals reflects the pattern of national demand to which the activities of citizens as producers must conform, if they are to secure collectively the greatest possible satisfaction from the resources available. Our observer in the central Planning Office could decide what ought to be produced to secure this satisfaction by observing in what way people were spending their incomes. If housewives decide to buy more milk and less bacon for their families, then the prices to be obtained for the present supply of milk will tend to rise, and grocers will find that at the current level of prices, stocks of bacon are accumulating, and they will order less from the bacon factories and press for lower prices. Prices link together demand and supply in such a way that supply at the current price tends to equal demand at the current price. A system of prices thus indicates the preference of consumers to which the pattern of supply should conform to secure the greatest possible amount of satisfaction, given the current distribution of income.

The division of resources between occupations created by the pattern of monetary demand within one country applies also in a modified form to the international market. If consumers can choose freely what goods to buy, they will tend to buy the cheapest goods that adequately fill their needs; as producers, they will offer such services as seem likely to bring the largest monetary returns, whether from home or foreign buyers. The wider the market, the greater are the benefits to be derived from specialised production based on natural resources in climate or minerals, or on inherited skills in hand or brain. In the nineteenth century, an international system of markets based on freely convertible sterling led to an international division of labour on a gigantic scale. In spite of the tariffs and exchange restrictions of the twentieth century, the economies of the United Kingdom and of New Zealand are still dominated by foreign trade; the standard of life of their populations depends very largely on the successful adjustment of their agriculture and industries to the changing demands of overseas markets.

Until 1914 it was generally accepted in Britain that (apart from a few special cases) the intervention of Governments in economic affairs was likely to arrest, rather than to promote, the continuing increase in the output of goods and services. Such matters as the control of animal diseases and the collection of agricultural statistics could usefully be undertaken by the State; but consciously to modify the size of any industry or the incomes earned by it was held to interfere with that proper mobility of resources between one use and another by which alone the nation would secure the greatest possible supply at the lowest possible cost. It was partly the war-time developments in administration and partly the economic confusion of the years after 1918 which led public opinion to allow to centralised Government a wider sphere of influence, including the maintenance of full employment, the provision of certain minimum standards of housing, medical care and education, and a general oversight upon economic development. To achieve the desired ends, Governments have relied largely on the manipulation of prices, using direct administrative measures to reinforce and supplement the effect of prices. The analysis of the persuasive and detailed influence of prices on all aspects of farming is therefore the first stage in the study of agricultural economics and of agricultural policies.

CHAPTER II

AGRICULTURE AND ECONOMIC DEVELOPMENT

Let us begin our study of agricultural policy and prices by considering the nature of the demand for agricultural produce, the part which agriculture plays in the economic life of various countries and the historical forces which have brought about the current situation. For such an analysis we shall need to equip ourselves with some economic concepts, beginning with the income-elasticity of the demand for food and the propensity to save.

I. INCOME-ELASTICITY OF DEMAND

As a nation or a group of people becomes richer, the demand for different products does not increase equally. Starting from a very low level of subsistence, the greater part of any increase in income will be used to obtain more food in total, or to obtain more of certain foods and thus to improve the content or variety of diet. At this level, the 'income-elasticity' of the demand for food is high; a rise of 10 per cent in income may induce more than a 10 per cent increase in the demand for food, and the demand for other commodities increases very little. But once the most essential demand for food is met, an increase in income will be used mainly to satisfy other wants and the expenditure on food will increase less than the rise in income; the income-elasticity of the demand for food will be less than 1.[1]

[1] The income-elasticity for a commodity can be defined as the percentage change in expenditure on that commodity divided by the percentage change in income which has caused that change in expenditure, other things being unchanged. Its precise measurement is difficult for various reasons. The definition of income is by no means easy, and total expenditure, which is more easily measured, need not closely follow changes in income. Changes in the expenditure on food may involve changes in quantities or in quality or in the amount of processing involved. But in spite of these problems of measurement the concept is useful.

Table 1. *Income-elasticity of demand for food*

	Food	Other	Total
If income-elasticity of demand for food exceeds 1			
Stage A	75	25	100
Stage B	84	26	110
Percentage increase	12	4	10
If income-elasticity of demand for food equals 1			
Stage A	75	25	100
Stage B	82½	27½	110
Percentage increase	10	10	10
If income-elasticity of demand for food is less than 1			
Stage A	75	25	110
Stage B	77	33	100
Percentage increase	3	32	10

The arithmetic of this relationship is set out above. It is assumed that at Stage A total income is 100 units, of which 75 are spent on food and 25 on other commodities; at Stage B income has risen by 10 per cent to 110 units.

Because the income-elasticity for food is less than 1 in most industrialised communities, the proportion of total income spent on food falls as income increases, a relationship sometimes known as Engel's Law. For instance, budgets collected from American families in 1941 showed the trend in the proportion of income spent on food reproduced in Table 2.

In Britain the income-elasticity for food in the years just

Table 2. *Proportion of income spent on food in the United States, 1941*

Net income class ($)	Spent on food Total ($)	Spent on food Percentage of income
under 500	144	49·7
500 — 1,000	272	36·9
1,000 — 1,500	402	32·4
1,500 — 2,000	521	30·0
2,000 — 3,000	693	28·3
3,000 — 5,000	849	24·0
5,000 and over	1,312	12·0

Source: Dewhurst and associates, *America's Needs and Resources* (Twentieth Century Fund, 1947), p. 98.

before the second world war appeared to be about 0·5 for the country as a whole, and in 1954-6 had fallen to about 0·3.[1] It was about 0·25 for the United States in 1941, where the average income commanded a larger amount of goods and services.

II. PROPENSITY TO SAVE

Our second analytical tool follows from another observation of the way in which most people use an increase in income. At the lowest level of subsistence, there is no saving, no appreciable difference between current income and current expenditure; people live from hand to mouth and are overwhelmed by minor misfortunes such as illness or crop failure. But at all levels of income except the lowest, some people (though by no means all) will try to accumulate a reserve in goods or money to carry them through the personal accidents of life, or to invest in their farm or business so as to secure a larger and more regular income in the future. The propensity to save from any increase in income for such purposes varies widely between different groups of people even at approximately the same levels of income; the desire for security in the future, the wish to have a larger income in the future, or to rise in the social scale, the possibility of extending a business, such factors depend partly on personality and partly on the whole social structure and the technical possibilities available. We cannot therefore predict what will be the propensity to save from an increase in income, except by a careful study of a group of fairly homogeneous people. A community with a high propensity to save can rapidly increase its stock of capital and its future income; a community with a low propensity to save will consume each year a high proportion of any increase in income and its stock of capital will therefore increase but slowly. If the first community secures, by any source, an initial rise in income, there can be a rapid rise in its stock of capital and in its potential income, available either for income or further investment; in the second community, an initial rise in income may peter out and may fail to create a continuous process of reinvestment and rising income.

[1] J. A. C. Brown, 'Seasonality and Elasticity of the Demand for Food in Great Britain since De-rationing', *J.A.E.*, vol. xiii, No. 3 (1959), pp. 228-41.

Equipped with these two concepts for analysis, let us consider the relationship between agriculture and other parts of the economy for a number of countries, as summed up in the concept of the national output of goods and services.

III. NATIONAL OUTPUT

The statistical problems of measuring the annual output of goods and services in any one country are formidable and complex; to compare the annual outputs of different countries adds further complexities. Even a comparison of the numbers employed in agriculture in different countries is no easy task. Agriculture is not one clearly demarcated trade, but a number of allied industries, combined in varying degrees, and ranging from commercial farms to mere pleasure gardens. In many countries, an agricultural occupation is often combined regularly or occasionally with other occupations, such as fishing, hunting, forestry, retail trading and various types of processing industry. Statistics of those gainfully employed in agriculture have thus a considerable margin of uncertainty, especially statistics collected by different countries for different purposes. But these difficulties of comparison, whether of national output or of employment, need not prevent us from using such information as does exist, provided we use it with common sense to indicate, not precise quantities, but the orders of magnitude involved.

Consider the statistics in Table 3, in which estimates of the annual value of the national output of goods and services for four countries are compared in terms of dollars.

Table 3. *Net national product in four countries, 1952-4*

	Net national product per capita		Percentage of personal expenditure spent on food	Percentage of occupied population engaged in agriculture
	$	% of U.S.A.		
U.S.A.	1,870	100	27	13
U.K.	780	42	31	6
France	740	40	44	25
Italy	310	17	47	44

Source: United Nations Statistical Papers, Series E, 4 (1957); 4H, 10 (1957).
F.A.O. *Yearbook of Food and Agricultural Statistics* (1958), vol. 1.

We deduce that most families in the United States could buy about five times as many goods and services as most families in Italy, more than twice as much as most French families, and twice as much as most British families. Families in America spent, on an average, one quarter of their income on a full and varied diet and had three times that sum left over for their other needs; Italian families spent, on an average, almost half their income on a much more monotonous diet.

The proportion of income which has to be spent on food, the first necessity of existence, is clearly an important indicator of comparative wealth. And since food is derived mainly from agriculture, the importance of agriculture, in countries without much foreign trade, varies roughly in proportion to their wealth. At one extreme, a country such as India, with a far lower level of income per head than those shown in the table given above, has 70-80 per cent of its population engaged in agriculture, mainly for the subsistence of the cultivators. The propensity to save is low, and the income-elasticity for food is high; a substantial part of any increase in income per head would be spent on buying more food.[1] The Italian families spent nearly half their incomes on food and about 44 per cent of the population was engaged in agriculture. The American families, spending one quarter of their income on food, were supported by 13 per cent of the population working on farms. These farm families produce so much more than the families in India or Italy, partly because they can command so much more land, capital and science; and the high output per man engaged in farming is one reason why the proportion employed in food production is so low.

IV. THE HISTORICAL EVOLUTION OF AGRICULTURAL OUTPUT

Dealing with the simplest case first, let us imagine a country which has no foreign trade and therefore no means of securing goods and services other than those it produces; let us analyse the stages by which such an economy can raise its standards of life, and pass from a subsistence agriculture to an industrialised

[1] F.A.O., *State of Food and Agriculture, 1957* (Rome, 1957), Part III.

community. The transformation occurred earliest in Britain among the major countries, and mainly in the century from 1750 to 1850; it occurred as the response of thousands of individuals to the opportunities offered them by new knowledge and new tools to improve their productive powers and increase their income. In much of the world today, the same transformation is being undertaken as a matter of deliberate policy by Governments, but whatever the method, the basic grammar remains much the same.

Looking mainly at the British example, and ignoring the part played in it by foreign trade, we can list the successive stages in the transformation as follows:

(i) An improved technical skill raises yields from existing land, or facilitates the cultivation of land hitherto unused, so that both total output and output per man employed in farming increases.

(ii) There is an increased supply of the basic foods at lower costs and lower prices.

(iii) The increase in food supply improves the diet of all sections of the population, and still leaves a margin of income for the purchase of other goods and services and for investment in the industrial equipment to make and transport them.

(iv) More food brings a fall in the death rate, especially among infants, which leads to a rise in population, some of which finds employment in satisfying the new demands for industrial goods and services. The towns growing up round these factories provide new markets for agricultural products.

(v) With a high propensity to save, the surplus income generated by the process of (iii) leads to a large investment in social and industrial capital such as canals, railways, roads, and fuel supplies. This equipment eventually yields a larger supply of goods at lower costs, thus making possible a continuous expansion in output and a continuous rise in income per head.

(vi) From this increasing investment, the efficiency of agriculture benefits by such things as better and cheaper transport, water supplies, fertilisers, machinery and power to drive it, the development of a banking system, of education and research. The supply of food continues to increase faster than the population.

(vii) There is a 'drift from the land', in the sense that all the rising generation born in country districts cannot obtain employment in agriculture, except at incomes much lower than those they could obtain in the new and expanding trades, to which a number of countrymen eventually move.

(viii) In so far as the community frees itself from the strait-waistcoat of an inadequate supply of food—a 'food problem', it runs into a 'farming problem'—the social problem of an agricultural community with lower incomes than those enjoyed by the urban groups.[1] The 'drift from the land' has in most countries not proceeded sufficiently fast to prevent a substantial and long-enduring disparity in incomes which becomes the basis of the traditional wage structure.

(ix) In a rapidly developing society, there is a strong pressure on individuals to follow the trend set by the leaders, and at least to maintain their social position by adding to their income, by accumulating capital or by reducing the number of children to be reared. This pressure exerted over the past century has contributed to a fall in the birth rate which has slowed down the expansion in population in much of Europe.

At the first stage in this process, land represents probably the most important source of wealth and certainly of economic and political power; the supply of food may be the most important single influence on the development and health of the community, limiting both the rise in population and the accumulation of capital. Until a hundred years ago, the fluctuations in the annual output of food from British farms dominated most other trends in the economy; the course of foreign trade, the volume of industrial employment, the sale of textiles, the marriage rate, all reflected the economic results of bad or good harvests.[2] At the end of the process, a community can become so rich that only a small proportion of its income is affected by changes in food prices, and the supply of food may have ceased to be a limiting factor in any sense.

Set out in this schematic and highly simplified form, we can

---

[1] T. W. Schultz, *Economic Organization of Agriculture* (New York, McGraw-Hill, 1953), p. 3.

[2] W. W. Rostow, *British Economy of the Nineteenth Century* (O.U.P., 1948), pp. 50-2.

perhaps understand how the importance of agriculture in a nation's life reflects not only the natural resources of that country, but also its present stage in this historical process of abolishing want in its crudest form. We can perhaps also detect some of the pitfalls which lurk between the various stages and which may so greatly hamper the process for some countries.

There are countries today where the race between agricultural improvement and increase in population is very narrow, where the propensity to save for future investment is low, because of the appallingly low incomes, and where the income-elasticity of the demand for food is high, for the same reason. In such countries, any increase in food supply serves to provide the same low standards of consumption for a larger population; under-employment in agriculture on a huge scale is combined with a shortage of capital which would enable that labour to be employed elsewhere. 'The curse of the poor is their poverty' applies most crucially in countries such as India and China, in which food supply is the regulating factor in economic development; here, the most urgent problems are those of agricultural improvements and education, land tenure, agricultural credit and of rural over-population and under-employment.

Even if an increase in population can be held in check, an initial impetus towards development caused by an improvement in food supplies may fade away if the community has a low propensity to save, if it consumes every year so much of the increased output that there is little surplus for investment. A government which conscientiously tries to lead its nationals through these various stages may have to impose 'forced' saving, to restrict the demand for consumer goods, if there is to be a substantial investment to secure further improvements in output in the future. The nineteenth century was in this respect more favourable to capital formation than the twentieth for countries undergoing the early stages of development. The public then expected less in the way of housing and social services; the business men who made the industrial and agricultural revolutions both kept the profits they made largely free of tax and also had a high propensity to save and to invest in their own businesses. But an attempt by the State to invest more than the community is willing to save is one explanation of the chronic tendency towards inflation which appears to accompany economic development in the modern world.

For the countries which have passed through the early stages in this historical process, agriculture has ceased to be the controlling factor in economic development; land, as such, is only a minute fraction of the national capital. Technical improvements and the application of science to the operations of farming have enabled these countries to obtain their food supply with a declining proportion of their resources in labour and capital. In such countries, a commercialised agriculture plays a subsidiary part in the economic life as a whole, and the conditions in which it operates are set by standards elsewhere. The process of industrialisation gradually breaks down the primitive distinctions between the various sectors of the economy; capital and labour tend to move more freely between regions, between industries and between social groups. And in such commercialised agriculture, the main problems are economic, not technical; farmers and their advisers are concerned with the maximisation of profits, not of output. Since this book deals mainly with such commercialised agriculture, the problems here considered are the terms of trade between agricultural and industrial products, the effect of technical improvements on the incomes of farmers, the factors which influence the distribution of capital and manpower between farming and other occupations.

V. THE INFLUENCE OF INTERNATIONAL TRADE

So far we have assumed that each country was a closed economy without access to foreign trade, an assumption which we must now discard; clearly, the part which agriculture plays in the economy of various nations is partly determined by the volume and direction of international trade. The facts that Britain has 6 per cent of her population engaged in agriculture and New Zealand has 21 per cent are related by a third fact— the export of agricultural products from the southern hemisphere to the northern, and the reverse flow of a wide range of industrial products. In the process of economic development, the opportunities of foreign trade may be of great importance in three ways.

If agricultural improvements that are limited and not cumulative induce a rapid rise in population, the production of a still greater food supply from a given area of land may become so costly that economic development may be checked almost at birth. The Law of Diminishing Returns was formulated by economists but it embodies a fact known to farmers all over the world; at a static level of technique, the application of successive units of capital or of labour to a given area of land will, after a point, yield diminishing returns in agricultural product. If we put this statement the other way round, we get that other generalisation from experience, the Law of Increasing Costs; at a static level of technique, successive units of agricultural output can only be secured from a given area of land at increasing costs in the input of other factors. The trend towards increasing costs is likely, of course, to be most conspicuous where agricultural technique is primitive and not easily changed, but it may act as a brake on development in any country where the population is increasing rapidly. In the last half of the nineteenth century, Britain was able to avoid these rising costs of her food supplies by the import of an increasing proportion from other countries, for which she exchanged her manufactured goods.

And secondly, these newly opened countries were helped over the stiffest part of their development by their ability to borrow from Britain the technical experts, the machinery and materials for railways and harbours without which they could not expand their economies. Instead of saving a large part of their income for investment, these countries borrowed the wealth of Britain, paying the annual charges out of that rising output which such investments made possible. Agriculture had a special role in the new countries of the nineteenth century, since the volume and value of agricultural exports was the basis of their ability to borrow during a critical stage.

And thirdly, agriculture remains for some countries the principal source of exports and therefore provides the principal means of paying for imports. Here again we may note three main factors which influence that specialisation of production on which international trade is based. There is firstly the variation between countries in climate, natural resources and inherited skills which makes it profitable to grow bananas in the West Indies but not in Scotland, and to weave tartans in Hawick but not in Trinidad. There is secondly the trend towards increasing costs which implies that densely populated countries may, after a certain level of agricultural production has been reached, find it cheaper to import their remaining requirements of food. And thirdly, there is the trend towards decreasing costs for certain industrial products as the scale of output increases, so that the larger the plant, the lower the costs per unit of output. The mass-produced car, American films, Swedish ball-bearings, British chemicals are examples of this type of specialisation, based on the economy of producing in large quantities for a large market. By this specialisation, each country is able to concentrate its resources on the production of those commodities for which it has a relative advantage; and all countries are able to have a wider variety of goods at lower costs than if each dwelt in splendid but squalid isolation. We shall return to this point again in a later chapter; here the relationships between agriculture and foreign trade are but briefly mentioned, as an explanation of the variable part which agriculture plays in the economic structure of different countries.

VI. THE TERMS OF TRADE

The standard of life of Robinson Crusoe depended at first on his own output, and then on the combined operations of himself and Man Friday, less the food consumed by the latter. If Man Friday had established himself on an adjacent island with a different soil and had grown different products, the standard of life of these primary producers would have depended firstly, on the output of each, and secondly on the terms at which they exchanged their different products. In a commercial society, the standard of life of persons and of groups similarly depends firstly on the volume of output each obtains, and secondly on the rate at which that output can be exchanged for all other goods and services. We each therefore have our own 'terms of trade'; on a larger scale, the terms of trade for a nation is a convenient shorthand expression for a comparison between the average price of its imports and the average price of its exports. In this Chapter, we shall use the 'terms of trade' to express the relationship between the average price which farmers as a group receive for their produce and the average price which they pay as a group for all the goods and services that they buy from the other sectors of the economy.

The longer the period over which we compare the terms of trade in this sense, the blunter and less useful becomes our tool. We are dealing here with large aggregates, whose composition changes over time. The total output of farms in the United Kingdom changed considerably in composition between 1900, 1925, and 1950, so that in talking of an average price in these years, we are in fact averaging different commodities in varying proportions. But within its own sphere of comparisons over a short period of time, the 'terms of trade' between agricultural and industrial products can be of assistance to us in analysing the changes in the value of agricultural output and incomes.

The purpose of our present enquiry is to consider the evolution of agricultural incomes in a developing economy. And by a developing economy we imply one in which resources of capital and technical knowledge are continually being invested in improving productivity both in agriculture and in industry. Output per man is increasing, let us assume at a steady rate of 2 per cent per year, so that both parties to the exchange between agricultural and industrial goods have more to offer year by year. If the terms of trade remained constant, then one composite unit of agricultural produce will exchange for one composite unit of industrial produce; the total value of both types of output will increase steadily and both parties will have a steadily increasing output and a steadily increasing income derived from the sale of that output at a constant rate of exchange. But can we expect that the terms of trade will remain unchanged?

VII. INCOME-ELASTICITY OF DEMAND AND THE TERMS OF TRADE

In fact, it is not likely that they will, because a nation whose real income is increasing has a falling income-elasticity in its demand for food, at all standards above the very poorest. As it gets richer, it will wish to spend more on food certainly, but the rate of increase is likely to be less than the rate of increase in income and in the demand for industrial products. So that if output per head is increasing at an equal rate in both agriculture and industry, the value of the total agricultural product is likely to fall relatively to the value of the total industrial product; the terms of trade are likely to move so that farmers must offer a greater quantity of agricultural products to secure the same quantity of industrial products. Those with industrial products to sell will be able to buy their necessary food at relatively lower prices, and they will thus be richer in two ways; they have a greater output to exchange and they can also secure more agricultural products for each unit of industrial product. The sellers of agricultural produce will also be better off in so far as they have more to offer on the market, but they will be worse off, in so far as each unit will exchange for a smaller quantity of the things they wish to buy. And it is conceivable that this second trend may outweigh the first, that the terms of trade may turn so sharply that a larger total of agricultural products will procure a smaller quantity of industrial goods and services for the farming community. Such circumstances, if continued, will result in a falling real income for this section of the community, while the industrial section secures a large increase in its real income.

Let us now take account of the various combinations between income-elasticity, technical progress and the terms of trade, which may lead to widely varying results in the distribution of income between the different sectors of the community.

The inhabitants of a poor country with a mainly primitive agriculture may wish to spend a considerable proportion of any extra income on food; their income-elasticity for food may be unity or possibly even higher. If technical progress in agriculture is less rapid than elsewhere, the supply of food may increase less rapidly than the demand for it, and the prices of food will then rise relatively to those of industrial products. In this case, the farming sector as a whole will obtain a relatively larger share of the slowly increasing income; the progress in the income of the industrial sector will be limited by the high cost of the basic foods. But as income rises, income-elasticity for food is likely to fall, so that a slower rate of technical progress in farming will suffice to maintain the previous terms of trade for the same population.

If technical progress is more rapid in farming than elsewhere and the supply of agricultural products increases at a faster rate than the supply of industrial goods, the industrial sector of the community will eventually benefit from the favourable terms of trade, the relatively lower prices for its food. However high the income-elasticity for food at the beginning, it is likely to fall as real income increases, so that each successive increase in the agricultural supply will meet a smaller proportionate increase in demand. In a wealthy community, therefore, technical progress in farming may lead rapidly to a fall in the aggregate value of farm output, and a fall in the aggregate income of the farming community as a whole. Perhaps the most unfavourable conjunction for the agricultural earners of income is a stationary and wealthy population and large technical improvements in agricultural processes, which, by greatly increasing output, might also quickly depress the aggregate value of farming income. It was some conjunction of this sort that contributed to that drastic shift in the terms of trade between agricultural and industrial products in world markets in the years between the wars.

Before we can proceed further, we must make these broad generalisations more precise. Firstly we must break up this single entity 'food' into its constituents and consider the varying demands for the different components of it; secondly, we must look at the relationship between the demand for these individual foods and the social distribution of income.

VIII. INCOME AND DIET

As people become richer, they spend on food a smaller proportion of their income but a larger sum; after a low level of income has been passed, that larger sum represents not a greater quantity of nutrients, but a shift from the cheaper and duller foods to the more expensive and tasty ones. At the lowest levels of income, expenditure is concentrated on the cheapest possible supply of calories obtained from a large consumption of starchy foods, such as cereals, rice, sugar, potatoes; to these is added a small quantity of supplements to provide palatability, fats, jam, tea and beer, the cheapest cuts of meat and fish. As income rises, there is a sharp rise in the expenditure on these supplements; when they form a substantial part of the total diet, the purchase of the starchy foods falls. At high incomes, the diets consist of expensive and protein-rich foods such as meat, poultry, fish, milk, eggs, butter, cheese, the expensive sources of vitamins—fruit and vegetables. The point can be illustrated from statistics on milk consumption at two periods, separated by more than twenty years and one world war (Table 4). At the first date, the consumption of milk was closely correlated with income, with a high income-elasticity for most groups. At the second date, full employment, higher wages for the hitherto lowest paid earners, childrens' allowances and cheap milk for mothers and babies have between them evened up milk consumption; income-elasticity for milk was estimated by Mr Empson to have fallen from 0·5 to 0·1 (a lower value than that shown in the more general survey of budgets).

Our concept of income-elasticity of demand requires one

Table 4. *Consumption of milk according to income in the United Kingdom, 1936/7, 1955*

1936/37		1955	
Annual income of head of household	Purchase of milk in pints per head per week	Weekly income of head of household	Purchase of milk in pints per head per week
£500 and over	5·1	£20 and over	5·8
£250—£499	4·4	£13—£20	4·9
£125—£245	2·6	£9—£13	4·5
under £125	1·6	£5— £9	4·2
		under £5	4·4

Source: J. Empson, 'Fresh Milk Market in England and Wales, 1939–1956', *J.A.E.* (1958), vol. XII, No. 3, pp. 349–60.

further qualification. At retail prices, consumers buy not only farm produce but also the capital, skill and time employed in processing, transport and storage. This development reaches its conclusion when urban families buy cooked meals in restaurants or factory canteens or from a deep-freeze unit in the local shop. In a wealthy community, much of any increase in expenditure on food is used to buy more processing of this sort, so that income-elasticity for the basic product is considerably lower than income-elasticity as measured at retail prices. But at current retail prices, household budgets collected in the United Kingdom between 1954 and 1956 indicated income-elasticities for the major foods of the magnitudes set out in Table 5.

Table 5. *Income-elasticity of the demand for foods in the United Kingdom, 1954-6*

Negative	Small positive	Medium positive	Large positive
Flour	Beef and veal	Cakes and	Poultry
Bread	Butter	biscuits	Coffee
Margarine	Cheese	Mutton and lamb	Fresh green
Dried peas and	Potatoes	Pork	vegetables
beans		Fresh milk	and legumes
Condensed		Cream	
skim milk		Condensed	
		whole milk	

Source: Adapted from Brown, *loc. cit.*

IX. DISTRIBUTION OF INCOME AND THE DEMAND FOR FOOD

The demand for food thus changes markedly with changes in income. Consequently, the total demand for various foods will change if the distribution of income in a community is altered, irrespective of any increase or decrease in the aggregate income. A community in which one family has £10,100 a year and 99 others have £100 each will spend its collective income quite differently from a society in which each family has £200, though the total income and the average income will be identical. And because the pattern of expenditure is different, the occupational pattern will also be different and the two societies will differ so markedly that their real income can hardly be compared. And there will be a third pattern of demand if the State removes £5,000 from the wealthy family as income tax, spends half of this on education and atomic bombs, and transfers the other half to the 99 poor families by way of children's allowances and old age pensions.

Any general redistribution in incomes will therefore cause considerable shifts in the relative strengths of demand between various agricultural products, and consequently may cause considerable changes in income accruing to different groups of farmers. For the agricultural economist, the national distribution of incomes within a community is a given fact, though as a citizen he may have opinions on what is desirable or practicable. In so far as he wishes to forecast the probable demand for agricultural products, he must work from the existing pattern, allowing for such modifications as he thinks likely to occur both in the aggregate income and in its distribution.

X. AGRICULTURAL POLICY AND ECONOMIC PROGRESS

Technical progress in agriculture and in industry implies a rising output and an increase in real income. In countries beyond the stage of primary poverty, a rise in real income is likely to bring about a slower rise in the demand for the basic foods than in the demand for many industrial products. If the increase in output occurs at about the same rate in agriculture and in industry, a relative fall is likely in the prices of farm produce. This fall in prices is, on the one hand, an essential part of the benefit obtained by economic progress, an essential part of the increase in real income for all buyers of food; on the other hand, the total income accruing to the growers of these products will increase less rapidly than the income of other groups in the community, and it may even fall in absolute size. The disparity in income is, in turn, an indication that fewer resources need to be devoted to food production, that some land, men and machinery can be more usefully and more profitably employed in providing other goods and services. In the face of such changes, can we lay down any principles for agricultural policy?

In the first place, a policy which aimed simply at maintaining the previously existing relationship between prices would contradict a policy of increasing the real wealth of a country, and would, indeed, ignore logic. Prices serve as indicators of the relative strengths of demand and supply in the various markets, which cannot remain unchanged in the process of economic development. The fact that demand alters as a nation gets richer implies that the relative importance of agriculture and industry, and of the different branches of farming itself, must also alter. If all changes in prices and in incomes from a pre-existent norm are to be prohibited, we shall have not a developing society but a static one, whose standard of living is for ever fossilised.

But if it is desired, in the interests of equality of incomes, to mitigate a severe fall in the incomes accruing to the growers of one group of commodities, we can encourage shifts in production within agriculture. If the demand for bread grains is rising less slowly than supply aided by science, and cereal prices are therefore falling on a long-term trend, agricultural policy can be directed towards the encouragement of dairy and livestock farming; the demand for milk, dairy produce and meat is likely to be strong at most levels of income and the growth of these industries may provide a secondary market for cereals. Or, alternatively, if cereal prices fall below the current level of those in international markets, it may be possible to develop an export trade, so that the fall is mitigated.

Finally, a relative or absolute fall in the total income accruing to agriculture need not create a corresponding fall in the income of individuals, provided the smaller total of income can be divided among fewer people. We may need to encourage the 'drift from the land', if we are seeking to equalise incomes, or to set free resources for the production of other commodities, not necessarily agricultural. Such policies cannot be combined with that of maintaining a given volume of employment in agriculture or the maintenance of a given number of peasant or family farms. If that is to be our main objective, then we must accept great disparities in income between workers in agriculture and workers in industry, or we must pay farm families special grants to keep them in their present employment and thus deter them from moving to other jobs where they would produce a greater value to the annual flow of goods and services. We shall return to this point later, when we are considering the structure of farming costs and the sizes of farms.

XI. SUMMARY

Let us now sum up the results of this discussion on the place of agriculture in a developing community.

As a society gets richer, its demand changes. Because demand changes, the relative importance of the occupations supplying these demands must also change. If a rapid rise in population is combined with a slow rise in productivity, especially in agriculture, the increase in real income per head will be limited by the relatively high prices for food; the greater part of the increasing wealth will accrue to the primary producers. If the rise in population is slow and the rise in productivity large, the increase in the demand for the basic foods may be lower than the increase in demands in other markets, their prices will lag behind other prices and the aggregate income accruing to their growers may not rise ; there may even be a fall in income per head in these branches of farming. The reaction to such changes must depend on the main objectives of agricultural policy, on the strength of public feeling in favour of a rapid rise in the average standard of life, of the maintenance of a previously existing distribution of income or some stated number of family farms.

Our discussion so far has dealt with what may be called long-term trends in agricultural prices and incomes; looking back at past decades, we can detect their influence more clearly then than we can amid the immediate distractions of current markets, whose fluctuations directly result from short-term situations. But farmers, consumers and Governments alike have to live in the short run, and we must now turn to consider the operation of markets and the fluctuations of prices which farmers are likely to meet from one year to another and even from one week to the next. Only then can we reasonably discuss the detailed operation of agricultural policies.

Further Reading

J. A. C. Brown, 'Seasonality and Elasticity of the Demand for Food in Great Britain since De-rationing', *J.A.E.* (1959), vol. XIII, No. 3.

F.A.O., *State of Food and Agriculture, 1957* (Rome, 1957), Section III.

J. R. Bellerby, *Agriculture and Industry, Relative Income* (Macmillan, 1956). (Mainly statistical.)

E. M. Ojala, *Agriculture and Economic Progress* (O.U.P., 1952).

W. A. Lewis, *The Theory of Economic Growth* (Allen and Unwin, 1955).

CHAPTER III

MARKET PRICES, DEMAND AND SUPPLY

So far, we have discussed the changes likely in a developing economy to affect the relative position of agriculture and of the other parts of the national structure. The next stage in our enquiry is to consider the working of agricultural markets in that short period in which we live and from which we have to deduce the long-term trends. In this chapter we shall consider the effect of demand and supply upon prices in the simplest of markets, in which producer and consumer are in direct contact; in the next chapter we shall modify our conclusions to take account of some of the complexities of distribution. For this next stage we shall require two tools—price-elasticity of demand and price-elasticity of supply.

I. PRICE-ELASTICITY OF DEMAND

Price-elasticity is indeed a fundamental concept for economic analysis of any sort. In the last chapter we used income-elasticity to describe how demand for any product was likely to alter with changes in income, other things remaining equal, including prices. Price-elasticity is the equivalent expression which sums up the change in the demand for any product caused solely by a change in the price of that product, other things remaining equal, including the level of incomes and the prices of all other products.

If a small change in price for one commodity produces a more than proportionate change in demand, then demand is said to be elastic, or to have a price-elasticity greater than 1. If a small change in price produces a less than proportionate change in demand, then demand is said to be inelastic, or to

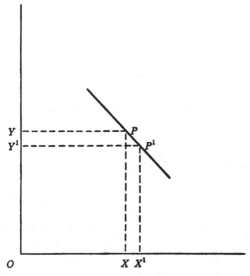

Fig. 1.   Elasticity of demand equal to unity.

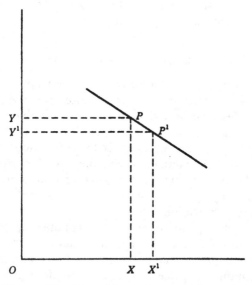

Fig. 2.   Elasticity of demand greater than unity.

have a price-elasticity of less than unity. Normally a change in price will produce a change in demand of the opposite sign; a rise in price causes a fall in demand, and a fall in price will lead to a greater demand. The relationship can thus be depicted graphically by a curve which slopes downwards from left to right; at any price, measured on the vertical axis, elasticity is measured by the slope of the curve for a small change on either side of that price. In Fig. 1, which represents the dividing line between the other two cases, a small change in prices produces, over the range of prices and sales here depicted, an equal and opposite change in demand. A fall of 2 per cent in price will produce a rise of 2 per cent in the volume of sales, that is, $\frac{XX^1}{OX} = \frac{YY^1}{OY}$. The importance of this case lies in the fact that as long as the demand has an elasticity equal to 1, the total receipts obtained from selling this commodity remain approximately equal; selling 100 units at a price of 100 each brings in approximately the same total as selling 98 units at 102 or 102 at 98.

On the other hand, Fig. 2 depicts the case where total receipts increase as the price falls and demand rises. A fall in price of 2 per cent here produces a rise in demand of more than 2 per cent; $\frac{XX^1}{OX}$ is greater than $\frac{YY^1}{OY}$. The purchasers collectively spend more as the price falls, so long as the elasticity is greater than unity. Fig. 3 shows the other type of demand in which the total receipts from the sale of the product fall as the price falls, because the rise in demand is proportionately less than the fall in price. Demand is inelastic, and so long as it remains inelastic, total receipts will fall with a falling price and rise with a rising price.

Price-elasticity expresses a relationship between a certain range of prices for one product and the corresponding levels of demand. We must distinguish between elasticity of demand and changes in demand which occur for other reasons than a change in price for that product. We can only put these other changes on our graph by drawing a new demand curve, expressing the new relationship between price and the changed demand. A successful advertising campaign brings about just such a change

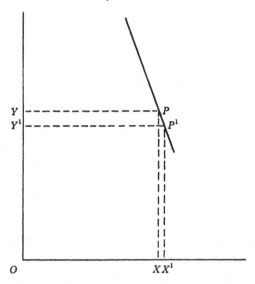

Fig. 3. Elasticity of demand less than unity.

in demand, so that at all levels of prices that can reasonably be foreseen demand will be greater; the new demand curve will then lie above and to the right of the former curve. If year by year, the British public drinks less beer, then year by year the demand for hops will fall, not along a demand curve, but from one demand curve to another, each demand curve lying below and to the left of the previous one, each demand curve expressing a temporary relationship between current demand and prices.

Later on, we shall look more closely at the forces which lie behind these graphs. Here we need make only three points. In the first place, the elasticity of demand for any product implies that we start from a known price level; the statement that a demand is elastic or inelastic implies a qualifying clause 'for a certain range of price'. At very high or very low prices, demand may play some odd tricks. Secondly, we have in these graphs eliminated time; we have assumed that a change in price produces its full effect on demand immediately, which is by no means always the case. Thirdly, we must specify the market to which our measurement of demand relates. If we assume that distributors, transport agencies and food manufacturers are remunerated for their services by a fixed sum—fixed over that period of time with which we are concerned—a given elasticity of demand at retail prices will be considerably reduced before it has worked through to the markets in which farmers sell.[1] Demand for farm products, being derived from the demand at retail prices, is likely therefore to have lower elasticities of demand than the markets in which consumers buy; the larger the processing margin, the greater will be the difference between the elasticity of demand at retail and at producer prices.

II. PRICE-ELASTICITY OF SUPPLY

Elasticity of supply is the expression which sums up the reaction of the supply of any commodity to a change in the price offered for it. The concept is mathematically clear, but its application to the problems of market pricing is complicated by the factors of time and technical change.

If we are considering the market for the week-end joint, then supply is rigidly fixed by the amount of meat already in the shops and in the wholesale stores in the urban centres; similarly, for livestock auction sales, the volume of supply is fixed by the number of beasts sent to each sale and prices will have to fall appreciably below the 'normal' level before farmers will reduce the supply by taking back unsold beasts, with the certainty of further costs to be incurred in feeding and in marketing at some later date. Because supply is fixed in this short period, the immediate level of prices is decided entirely by the strength of demand. We can depict such a situation graphically by a vertical line as a supply curve; the final price will reflect the volume of demand and will change with it.

[1] Suppose 100 units sell at 100 each at retail prices;
　　but 105 units sell at　90 each

then e at retail prices $= \dfrac{5}{100} \bigg/ \dfrac{10}{100} = 0\cdot5.$

Assume processing margin of 45; then at wholesale prices,
　　100 units sell at 55 each;
　　but 105 units sell at 45 each;

then e at wholesale prices $= \dfrac{5}{100} \bigg/ \dfrac{18}{100} = 0.28.$

If however we are considering the supply of meat in the month of December, we have to recognize that supply may vary from day to day, as a result partly of farmers' expectations of prices; in other words, there will be some elasticity of supply. If prices in December are high and farmers expect them to fall after Christmas, the supply in December may be increased by the marketing of beasts that could have been held until January. Supply in December can then be graphed by a line sloping up from left to right, indicating that as prices rise, so supply will be increased. The increase cannot be large in any one month, since the amount is limited by the number of beasts approaching an acceptable degree of fatness and by the existing stocks of meat ashore and afloat. Over a period of, say, two years, the supply of beef is still limited by the existing number of calves and is therefore only moderately elastic. But in the same period the supply of pigmeat can alter markedly, because of the short periods of gestation and of fattening, so that the supply over two years is highly elastic to a change in the expected price of pigmeat. As a general rule, the longer the period, the more elastic is supply, the response varying with the technical factors on which that supply depends.

A discussion of these factors must be deferred to a later chapter, but it must be noted that supply curves of the type drawn here over-simplify the picture in assuming that the process of expansion or contraction is reversible. That is perhaps a reasonable assumption with a product like pigmeat, where the elasticity of supply is large in the short period; but for beef, the technical conditions determining the degree of elasticity are likely to change within one cycle of expansion or contraction. And finally, we must distinguish between elasticity and variability of supply. *Elasticity* is the aggregate result of a number of reactions to an actual or expected change in the price of any product, other things remaining equal. *Variability* of supply includes all the other changes which arise either from technical developments or from the accidents of weather and disease. But if a large variation in output creates a change in market prices, then we may find elasticity of supply coming into play, in answer to the change in prices; the two changes, though logically distinct, are in practice closely connected.

III. VARIABLE SUPPLY

Equipped with these tools, let us consider (rather in the abstract) the mutual interaction of supply, demand and price in the kind of markets which are important to farmers. As a start, let us assume a competitive market in which farmers and consumers deal direct with each other. They need not all be in one place provided there is a sufficient flow of market intelligence for each buyer and seller to be aware of the current level of prices.

If the supply is variable, in the sense given above, and the demand inelastic, we shall get widely fluctuating prices and an even greater variation in the aggregate receipts of producers. The statistics of yield, output and price of potatoes indicates this conjunction, which is common to the markets of many perishable products. Table 6 shows that British producers sold in 1956/7 slightly more and obtained lower total receipts than in 1955/6 or 1957/8 when the crop was smaller by about one million tons. This type of fluctuation in prices and incomes will, of course, average out over a short run of years; the established potato grower should plan his output, not by the price ruling when he orders his seed, but by the average of prices over the past three or four years, covering the normal variations in yield. But it has been shown by statistical analysis that between 1920 and 1935 plantings in Britain did in fact reflect the

Table 6. *Maincrop potatoes sold for human consumption in the United Kingdom, 1955/6 to 1957/8*

1955/56		1956/57		1957/58	
Tons (000)	£ (m)	Tons (000)	£ (m)	Tons (000)	£ (m)
3,400	64·6	3,750	41·25	3,440	71·7

Source: *Report of the Potato Marketing Scheme, year ended 30 June, 1958*, p. 9.

seasonal variations in prices; high prices because of low yields in one year encouraged farmers to plant more than usual for the next harvest, although there was no reason to expect another low yield. This type of irrational response, this elasticity of supply to chance variations in price, is one reason why such price fluctuations are undesirable, and are now often mitigated

35

by organised control, as for potatoes in this country.[1] But it is the huge variations in income which make these price variations so unpopular with producers of crops. With an inelastic demand, quite a small increase in output can, in a competitive market, bring about a substantial fall in price and greatly reduce the total receipts. If farmers set up some marketing organisation which can hold back the surplus over average yields, then the price should not fall below the 'normal' level, though it will still rise above it in times of scarcity. Is this type of market control to be recommended, or should we condemn it as against the public interest?

The fall in prices in a year of high yield occurs because the sellers compete with each other to satisfy a demand which increases only slightly with a fall in price. Nevertheless, that fall in price does lead to some increase in consumption, which would otherwise not have occurred. To prevent a fall in price means that a higher proportion of the product is wasted, or is diverted to a use of lower value. Further, to prevent that fall in price prevents also that improvement in real income for consumers which follows when the normal supplies of a basic foodstuff can be obtained with a smaller total of expenditure, leaving a surplus for other goods. The larger the proportion of expenditure devoted to this product, the more substantial is the general benefit foregone if good yields are never to be reflected in lower prices. Wherever the product concerned plays an important part in the ordinary diet, we should consider whether the benefit obtained by consumers from the low prices induced by a high yield outweighs the loss to producers.

There are also other ways than price control to obtain a fair stability in incomes. Farmers can sell a variety of produce, whose yields are not likely to vary in the same direction at the same time. One of the great benefits conferred by the normal crop rotations in Britain is summed up in the well known proverb

> Either the rain is destroying the grain,
> Or the drought is wrecking the roots.

---

[1] R. L. Cohen, *Factors affecting the Price of Potatoes in Great Britain*. Dept. of Agriculture, Farm Economics Branch, Report No. 15 (Cambridge, 1930).

T. W. Gardner, 'Cereal Prices and Acreages', *J.A.E.* (1957), vol. XII, No. 3, pp. 361–70.

Variability in agricultural incomes from individual markets can be largely ignored if that income is only a small fraction of the total receipts of most farmers who generally practice a diversified type of farming. But we must also recognise that there are large groups of single-crop farmers—growers of coffee or rubber or wheat—whose incomes show great variability; and there are countries whose export trade is dominated by one or other of these crops. A large fall in aggregate receipts caused by the attempt to sell on international markets an unusually large crop may seriously disturb the foreign exchange markets and impede the normal flow of imports. A Government may regard with equanimity a temporary redistribution of income between its own citizens which it cannot favour when the citizens of another country obtain the benefit from lower prices, or when the low prices cause acute difficulties in the financing of international trade.

If the product is one that can be stored from one season to the next at no great cost, then a programme of storing the surplus of a good year will probably benefit both producers and consumers. The loss of income to producers in years of glut will be prevented as well as high prices and scarcity when yields are low. 'The ever-normal granary', buttressed by stores accumulated in favourable seasons, is an obvious target for agricultural policies.[1] But difficulties arise because the process of accumulation and dispersal takes place within an economy which is itself changing; the 'average' price which should control the flow into and out of storage is itself changing because of technical developments in supply or changes in demand. Experience of commodity control schemes in the years between the wars showed how difficult it was to avoid a continuing accumulation of stocks which eventually wrecked their main purpose, that of price stabilisation. The theory is simple; the practice is beset with difficulties in organisation, in finance, in administration.

Milk is an interesting case of a perishable product with a variable supply, the markets for which have been brought increasingly under control, for a number of reasons. Governments have been concerned to ensure for consumers a regular supply

[1] Gen. xli.

of a food which has both a high nutritional value and a high risk of contamination with a variety of dangerous germs. The output must therefore come from producers with approved equipment and it has to be channelled through approved processes, pasteurisation and refrigerated transport, into bottles or waxed cartons at the point of retail sale. In the short period, the final demand for milk is usually inelastic to a fall in price, so that a casual surplus may depress prices very considerably. When towns were small and public health requirements less rigorous, producers retailed their own milk, and adjusted their variable supply to the demand by converting the seasonal surplus into butter and cheese. But as towns grew and began to draw their milk from a wider area, milk processing and distribution required expensive plant and retailing came to be organised in large units, whose profits were vulnerable to 'undercutting' by those with a seasonal surplus of milk, no manufacturing capacity and possibly lower standards of hygiene than were desirable. Recurrent price wars among distributors may have benefitted consumers for short periods, but they might also force down producer prices to the point where output fell and consumers might be deprived of milk in the next period of seasonal shortage. Hence in most industrialised countries, the prices of liquid milk have been controlled either by Government regulation or by agreement between distributors, under Government sanction; the seasonal variability in output has been concentrated on to the output of milk products and hardly affects the price structure for liquid milk which only slowly reflects the changes in demand, in supply, or in distributive costs.

IV. VARIABLE DEMAND

If the supply of a product is inelastic in the short period and can only be adjusted to price changes after a considerable time, changes in demand may again create widely fluctuating prices. The international wool market provides an illustration, on a gigantic scale, of the effect on prices of a variable derived demand and a supply which is virtually inelastic for a year or more and shows only a low elasticity thereafter (Table 7).

Table 7. *Price index of Dominion wools at London, 1947–52*

	Merino 64's	Crossbred 50's
1947/8	100	100
1949 Sept.	109	117
Dec.	134	159
1950 March	157	173
June	173	191
Sept.	254	415
Dec.	276	452
1951 March	387	673
June	208	327
Sept.	138	194
Dec.	168	224
1952 March	136	155
June	160	185
Sept.	158	206
Dec.	169	215

Source: Commonwealth Economic Committee, *World Consumption of Wool*, 1950–53, p. 31; 1952–56, p. 24 (H.M.S.O.).

The start of the Korean war in June 1950 led to an enormous purchase of clothing and blanket wools by the United States and other belligerents, in a market whose supplies were virtually inelastic; the rise in prices was exaggerated because in the short period the demand for a non-perishable industrial raw material is positively elastic—it tends to rise with a rise in prices as the consuming trades attempt to buy future requirements before prices rise further. Demand was only checked when enough trade buyers decided that the ultimate consumer would not buy enough of the product to be manufactured from the expensive wool to make continued buying profitable. Estimates of the elasticity of demand for the final product provide therefore the ultimate check on rising prices, but in the case depicted in the table given above, prices rose 4 to 6 times the pre-1950 level before demand was choked off, the rise in prices halted and then reversed. Once a price fall begins for a product like this, demand again proves positively elastic, buyers at first holding off the market in the hopes of still lower prices; the fall is checked only when accumulated stocks have been used and some buyers feel that prices will fall no further.

This type of derived demand partly explains the very large fluctuations in prices which can occur in wholesale markets for durable commodities. Yet such price changes do eventually equate demand to immediately available supply, either by encouraging consumers to buy more of the temporarily plentiful commodity or by rationing demand to the temporarily scarce supply. If prices are not to be allowed to function in this way, then some other mechanism has to be created, a rationing scheme for a period of scarcity, storage or destruction for the unexpected surplus. These administrative measures are necessarily slow to initiate, cumbersome in working and often costly in manpower. But for a basic foodstuff on which consumers spend an appreciable part of their total expenditure, we might favour low prices in times of glut, plus rationing rather than extreme high prices in times of acute scarcity, provided the average return over a period induces a supply adequate for most years. Where the product provides the main source of income for a large group of specialised growers and is not important to any appreciable number of consumers, we might perhaps favour some administrative control over a temporary and unexpected surplus, rather than a precipitate fall in price.

V. PRICE AND UTILITY

Demand changes with price because the final buyers habitually consider how to get 'value for money'. Let us, by way of illustrating the phrase, assume that our community is composed of identical individuals spending from compulsorily equalised incomes. If our consumers are rational, they will each of them spend their incomes to secure the greatest total of satisfaction; the optimum stage of bliss will be reached when each person will not get more satisfaction by spending at current prices one pound less on milk and one pound more on beer. This satisfaction or marginal utility to be derived from each line of expenditure obviously depends both on the market price of the product (which determines what quantity the consumer gets for his pound) and on the quantity which the consumer already owns; the more we have of any product, the less urgently do we need another unit, and the lower the marginal utility of that extra unit. Bread may be the staff of life, but to the economic planner the question is how much bread, how much butter and how much jam will provide the maximum satisfaction to those who are planned? Given the current market prices, only the consumers can decide whether the marginal utility of another pat of butter is less than the marginal utility of another slice of toast, or whether they would prefer to pile the butter more thickly on the same number of slices and spread the jam more thinly. If prices are free to move, the volume of consumer expenditure on each product will influence the level of market prices, and indicate whether, from a given situation, more butter is needed more urgently than more jam.

The same argument holds in a less rigorous form if we now remove our initial assumptions, if we allow our community to consist of infinitely variable human beings with a considerable inequality in incomes. We cannot in these circumstances assume equality in marginal utility for the expenditure on milk of Mr A with £5,000 a year and of Miss B, an elderly vegetarian living on a pension counted out weekly in shillings. Mr A can probably afford the luxury of not calculating strictly what marginal utility he derives from his expenditure on milk and his demand is likely therefore to be inelastic to price changes. But Miss B is likely to allot her income fairly strictly to secure equal marginal utility from the last shilling spent on each main product; she will quickly shift her demands if there is a change in milk prices and therefore in the utility obtained from a shilling's-worth of milk. It is this weighing up of marginal utility as prices change, these shifts in purchases by thousands of consumers in order to equalise their marginal utility which make up the demand curves depicted earlier. And it is these thousands of individual judgments of the comparative value at current prices of rather more of this and a little less of that which provide the ultimate facts to which planners and producers must eventually conform.

VI. IMPERFECT COMPETITION

We have spoken of competitive markets, but this term must now be made more precise. Perfect competition can be defined as a market in which no single buyer or seller can, by his own action, influence the current market price. For each individual, supply or demand can be represented as a horizontal line, implying that any amount is available at the ruling price for a buyer, and that demand at the ruling price is unlimited for a seller. Each seller can sell all his output at the current price for that quality; he is unlikely to get a higher price. Each buyer can buy all he wants at the current price; he is unlikely to find a seller who will take less. Each seller in planning his output takes the expected average price as given fact, to which his plans must conform; that average market price is determined by the interaction of aggregate demand and aggregate supply, to which each individual buyer and seller contributes only an insignificant fraction. In the nature of things, some expectations out of a large number will prove eventually to have been unduly optimistic or pessimistic, and prices may at times move almost irrationally as a consequence. Nevertheless, these short oscillations centre on that equilibrium price at which total demand and supply are equal. Each buyer and each seller must decide what quantity should be bought or sold at current prices, since the quantity demanded or offered is the only factor which the individual can control.

Where competition is less than perfect, then by definition individual buyers or sellers have to consider the effect of their own actions on the market in which they operate. Let us assume a market in which a large number of buyers trade with a comparatively small number of sellers. To each of these sellers demand appears as a curve with various kinks at prices where competition becomes acute. It may be that each seller has a strong position in a particular locality and meets with competition only on the boundaries, as with many producer-retailers; or each seller may have developed his own brand for which he has a select ring of clients. In either case, each seller finds that at the top of the range of prices, competition becomes effective and sales fall off sharply; at the lower range (if costs

Table 8. *Marginal revenue to a seller*

Units offered for sale	Price	Total revenue	Marginal revenue
70	11½	805	—
80	11	880	+75
90	10½	945	+65
100	10	1,000	+55
110	9	990	−10

can be reduced so far) one seller can capture a substantial fraction of the total demand. Between these two limits, the volume of sales by each seller will itself be one of the factors in determining his price, so that in planning his production he must take into account his 'marginal revenue', or the change in total receipts produced by a change in sales. For instance, let us assume that one seller finds a demand as depicted in Table 8. In such a market the seller will not normally sell more than 100 units at a price of 10 each; if he sells more, his total receipts will fall, and as it is unlikely (though not impossible) that his total costs should be less for a larger quantity, profits would also fall with a fall in price. In such markets, sellers normally proceed by deciding on a price for their product and then waiting to know what volume of sale results; they are price-fixers and quantity-takers (in Mr Wiles' useful phrase)[1] while sellers in perfectly competitive markets are price-takers and quantity-fixers. It is a common complaint of primary producers that they, alone among the sellers in an industrial environment, cannot set their own prices; such a complaint ignores the fact that price-fixers must be prepared to cope with unsold stocks, short-time working and financial loss because sales are less than planned capacity.

It is obviously to the interest of each seller in a market of this sort to make his product as much unlike that of his competitors as possible; if the buyers think that there is no difference between A's output and B's, a small difference in price may cause a large transference of demand. But if buyers think that B's brand is a rather poor substitute for A's, then A has a wider range of price within which to manœuvre before his sales are substantially affected by the price or quality changes of his

[1] P. Wiles, *Price, Cost and Output*, p. 4. (Blackwell, 1956.)

competitors. Hence much of the high-powered and expensive advertising of firms selling branded products, by which they hope not only to raise the total sales of the industry as a whole but to create a special market for their particular brand of it. And this also is a practice of little use in the more competitive markets in which farmers sell, though it has been used to build up markets for small specialities such as Channel Island milk with its high fat content, farmhouse cheeses, table poultry and some fruits and vegetables.

In a market where competition is very imperfect, a seller may be able to increase his sales by selling to isolated groups of buyers at different prices, in accordance with his estimates of the elasticity of demand in each market; he may by this means achieve a greater output and greater profit than if he sold at substantially the same price to all buyers. Such a policy is likely to be unpopular unless there are socially accepted reasons for the discrimination; cheap milk for mothers and babies does not now arouse ill-feeling among those outside these groups, but there might be considerable ill-feeling if cheap milk was confined to red-haired mothers and left-handed children. In the international sphere, a sales policy of this sort is called dumping and is regarded as unsporting, partly because it is usually only a temporary phenomenon which may inflict damage to the sales of competing producers while it lasts. (It is of course perfectly logical for any seller to quote local prices which vary because of the cost of transport from the nearest point of manufacture; indeed, to sell at uniform prices over a wide area served from one producing unit implies imperfect competition in some markets, which enables the 'discriminating monopolist' to make a varying profit margin above his distributing costs).

Similarly, if there are only a few buyers dealing with a large number of competing but ill-informed sellers, then each buyer may find that he can buy a certain quantity rather under the long-period market price, but that as he extends his purchases into areas better served with competitors, the marginal cost to him of the extra units may be very high, and he may refrain from buying. If he finds that on buying 110 units rather than 100, the price per unit which he must pay rises from 10 to 12, then the marginal cost to him of the ten extra units will be 320; his need must be urgent before he pays so high a price. Hence the limited market for farm produce often found in areas of poor transport inadequately served by wholesale firms. This point has importance also for the large buying organisation, whether Governmental or commercial; it may often be cheaper to buy extra quantities from an outside source at a price slightly above the internal or local price, if the alternative is to force that price sharply upwards for the total volume of purchases. If such a buyer can in fact buy at different prices in different markets, then he becomes, in the economist's jargon, a 'discriminating monopsonist', again liable to unpopularity but again socially acceptable in certain circumstances. And in the extreme case, a sole buyer or seller, facing a large number of unorganised competitors for his custom, may be able in the short run to compel them to accept individually negotiated prices designed to extract from each the greatest profit for the holder of monopoly power. But such a policy is likely to be successful for only a short time; retaliation takes the form either of governmental control of charges or of organisation among the unorganised competitors.

We have so far discussed perfect and imperfect competition in highly abstract terms; in the next chapter this skeleton must be given some life in the setting of modern agricultural markets. But even at this level of abstraction, it should be clear that a high degree of imperfect competition among either buyers or sellers is apt to produce a like movement on the other side. Monopoly, like mumps, is infectious. If the half-dozen buyers in a trade are holding off the market because buying more will raise prices against themselves, if they are to some extent acting as discriminating monopsonists, then there is a strong inducement for the sellers to set up a single selling agency to do their bargaining for them. And similarly, if there are only a few sellers suspected of joint action to restrict output in order to raise prices, then the unorganised buyers will rapidly organise as far as possible. But when two monopolists settle prices by direct negotiations, the outcome is, within limits, indeterminate; it is the student of diplomacy or applied psychology rather than the economist who is best qualified to predict the result and to analyse the process by which it has been reached.

The determination of prices in agricultural markets is thus a matter of vast complexity. In any market there is firstly the volume of immediate demand and the level of immediate supply; there are the influences percolating from other markets which affect demand, as a shortage of butter affects the demand for margarine. There is the variability of supply from day to day or from month to month, according to the technical conditions of production and storage; there is the structure of each market, the number and importance of individual buyers and sellers, while the historical development of each trade leads to special customs and conventions. But behind all these conflicting forces, each with its own influence of the day-to-day price, lies the trend in demand and supply to which the general trend in the price of any commodity must eventually conform.

If we have a crop with a variable supply and an inelastic demand, we must expect in a free market widely fluctuating prices. If in addition the income-elasticity for such a product is low while its output is rising because of technical improvements in production, then such price fluctuations will occur about a falling trend in price which should discourage any substantial increase in the area planted. Producers will complain of continuously low incomes, only occasionally relieved by a year of low yields and moderately high price; falling prices will constantly tend to outrun the fall in costs by which producers try to offset their falling incomes. This kind of situation can be depicted graphically as in Fig. 4, where supply increases from SS through S^1S^1 to S^2S^2 while demand only rises from DD to D^2D^2; on a free market we should expect price fluctuations round a falling trend from P to P^1 to P^2. But there is bound to be pressure for the fixing of a minimum price enforced perhaps by a monopoly seller; any price held consistently above the long-term trend will need to be buttressed by some type of production control which in turn may freeze the pattern of supply as it existed at some particular date. Alternatively, if the commodity is one for which both price and income-elasticity is high, then the short fluctuations in market price may occur

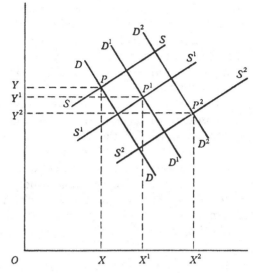

Fig. 4. Slowly rising demand with increasing supply.

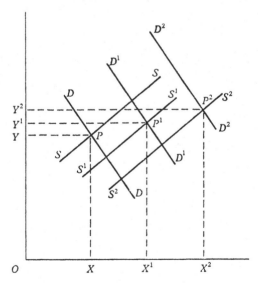

Fig. 5. Rapidly rising demand with increasing supply.

against an upward trend in average prices, as from P to P^1 to P^2 in Fig. 5. There may be occasional years of low prices caused by high yields, or by large technical improvements in production which suddenly stimulate supply, but any fall in profits is likely to be temporary and a stronger market will gradually absorb the larger output.

If, then, producer prices are judged too low to provide what is regarded as a reasonable income, or retail prices to consumers are judged to be too high for the incomes of the poorest, remedial measures must be adapted to the underlying forces which determine the long-term trend in prices and not merely to the surface phenomena. And reformers also need to be well acquainted with the market structure through which products pass from the farmers to the consumers since the intricacies of that structure also influence the process of price formation.

Further Reading

H. D. Henderson, *Supply and Demand* (C.U.P., 1922).

P. A. Samuelson, *Economics: An Introductory Analysis* (McGraw-Hill, 1948).

A. W. Stonier and D. C. Hague, *A Textbook of Economic Theory* (Longmans, 1953).

CHAPTER IV

MARKETING OF AGRICULTURAL PRODUCE

The various processes included under marketing in the modern world may be classified under seven heads:[1]

1. Assembly.
2. Grading and packing.
3. Transport over space.
4. Transport over time—storage or preserving.
5. Processing.
6. Finance and insurance.
7. Risk-taking (a) of physical deterioration.
   (b) of price changes.

Not all commodities undergo all these stages. For some, transport may involve shipment from one end of the world to the other, with all the consequential processes of preservation and finance; for others, transport may involve no more than a van to the nearest market stall. The food distributive trades present a wide variety of practices and customs, originating partly in the varied technical qualities of the products concerned, partly through historical and geographical factors. In some trades, producers, collectively or individually, own the product until bought by the final consumer; in others, processors buy the raw material direct or through merchants and finance all stages up to the retail shop; in others, a number of intermediaries provide specialised functions in getting the product from thousands of producers to thousands of consumers, perhaps in a much altered form.

I. TRANSPORT COSTS AND MARKETS

In most parts of Britain, the distributive trades evolved with the growth of towns on the one hand and the commercialisation

[1] E. Thomas, *Introduction to Agricultural Economics* (Nelson, 1949), pp. 234–9.

49

of farming on the other, as part of an expanding and highly competitive economy. A merchant's business grew because he could offer his customers better prices or more convenient services at lower costs than his competitors. His skill in buying and selling, the expert knowledge that minimised the risks of changing markets, enabled him to perform the varying functions of a distributor at a reasonable profit to himself and with reasonable satisfaction to those with whom he traded. The unsuccessful merchants performed, for a time, the same functions, but either their costs were higher, their service inadequate, or at some stage they took a risk which turned out unfavourably.

Every improvement in communications, every reduction in the cost of transport, has stimulated a double trend in agricultural marketing. The introduction first of canals, then of railways, then of road transport and telephones, served to break down the partial seclusion of local markets and to create more effective competition. Individual farmers or distributors might lose or gain in the process; national groups of farmers might lose their partial monopolies; but farmers collectively as well as consumers gained from these wider and less variable markets. In the decade after the first world war, for instance, dairy farmers serving local towns found their market increasingly invaded by distant producers whose milk could be brought direct by road; milk prices in consequence tended towards greater equality over the country as a whole, with the farms distant from towns gaining and those near to towns losing on balance.[1] This integration of markets, this intensified competition and more uniform price structure was accompanied by a second trend, towards amalgamation among the food processors and distributors. Each improvement in transport enabled the enterprising firm to cover more territory and to handle a larger volume of business without appreciably more effort. Then also the introduction of new processes often involved large units to secure the most economic size—plants for pasteurising milk, factories for bacon curing, butter and cheese manufacture, compounding plant for fertilisers and feeding-stuffs, grain driers and silos for the crops increasingly sold, after

[1] For the international aspects of falling transport costs, see Chapter VIII.

the second war, straight from the combines. The increase in the most economic size of these plants also increased the cost and risk of entering these trades, so that competition from new firms became progressively less effective. Thus as markets became larger and more uniform the number of firms operating at some particular stages showed a marked decline. From the 1935 Census of Production a calculation has been made of the 'degree of concentration' then existing in a number of trades of importance to farmers, either as suppliers of agricultural requisites or as purchasers of agricultural products (Table 9).

Table 9. *Degree of concentration in some U.K. industries, 1935*

	Percentage of gross output from three largest firms
Wheat, port mills	61
Preserved meat and fish	57
Pickles, sauces, condiments	53
Sausages	56
Condensed milk	93
Spirit distilling	76
Oilseed crushing	78
Soil and drain pipes	60
Matches	95
Rubber tyres and tubes	70
Cement	72

Source: H. Leak and A. Maizels, 'Structure of British Industry', *J.R.S.S.* (1945), vol. cviii, pp. 186–99.

Imperfect competition may therefore be regarded as common in many of the markets in which farmers sell their products and buy their requirements; the economy of large-scale processing and trading, the cost and risk of establishing new firms, the general reduction in transport costs, have all helped over decades to leave only a few firms operating in these trades. But the extent of this imperfection must not be exaggerated. For example, the immediate customers of grain sellers are the scores of produce merchants operating from county towns; by car or by telephone, farmers can quickly obtain competitive quotations for any sizeable quantities of grain or certified seeds or potatoes. The larger livestock auctions also provide highly competitive markets for a product of varying quality; here, again, road transport has probably improved competition since it has led to a concentration of business at the larger and more convenient markets; there has been a corresponding decay in some of the smaller auctions in which buyers and sellers were sometimes too few to provide an active market. Specialised vegetable merchants also offer an effective demand in most rural districts and form the link between the vegetable growers and the large urban wholesale markets which set the current price level.[1]

II. PRODUCER-RETAILING

Logically, the simplest market is that in which the grower sells his own product to the final consumer with no intermediary. In primitive communities, such retail markets often provide the main outlet for the produce of most growers and they may exhibit a high degree of imperfect competition, created by the small numbers of buyers and sellers, the lack of market intelligence, the variability of local supply, as well as by custom, caste or absence of trading finance. But direct contact between growers and consumers ceases to be possible when towns grow big and their food supplies must be drawn from outside the range of daily or weekly visits. In Britain today, most farm produce is sold to a wide variety of specialised merchants or processors; only a small volume of eggs, fruit and vegetables and table poultry is sold direct from the farm. Even for these transactions the prices are usually settled by reference to those obtained in the large wholesale markets for comparable produce so that local variations in supply or demand have only a limited influence on local prices.

III. SELLING ON CONTRACT

Selling on contract implies an undertaking to supply a stated quantity at stated times for an agreed price. The contractor undertakes the risk of finding a market for that quantity at a price which will satisfactorily cover his costs of buying, holding

[1] *Report of the Committee on Horticultural Marketing* (H.M.S.O., Cmnd. 61, 1957).

or processing. Included in his costs are the substantial risks that he runs during the period of the contract—risks that his forecast of the ultimate demand may prove to have been wrong, that his competitors may find a cheaper source of supply; alternatively there may be higher returns than were expected. Both parties to the contract take risks of unforeseen changes in costs during its currency; the farmer must also allow for some unplanned changes in output which may make it difficult to deliver precisely the stated quantities at the agreed time, he may have to buy in supplies to fill his contract, or pay a penalty for partial default, or dispose of a casual surplus in some other market. In many ways this might be regarded as the best method of marketing; farmers have one annual bout of bargaining and can then get on with their business of production. Yet only a fraction of the produce of British farms is sold by this method—sugar beet, some bacon pigs (indirectly through the Fatstock Marketing Corporation), farm seeds and some vegetables or fruit sold for processing.

In the first place, the variability of supply of agricultural products makes it difficult for growers to enter into the type of precise contract favoured by the processing trades. For crops, growers can only offer the produce of a certain area to be delivered at unpredictable times, according to the forwardness or lateness of the season. The output of livestock products may be more evenly spread over the season but may again be highly variable over short periods. The processors may well find that a level supply is best secured if they buy part of their requirements only on contract and buy the remainder as required in the open market. But individual contracts have proved useful in inducing farmers to take up new crops, such as sugar beet or flax; and before 1932 most of the urban milk supply was bought from farmers on individual annual contracts either by distributors or by the creameries.

In the second place, a farmer selling on contract sells in a highly imperfect market, since the suppliers of agricultural products are almost always much more numerous than the processors, and usually much less well informed on market trends and prospects. There is thus a strong tendency for those selling on contract to set up a single bargaining authority to negotiate terms and prices on their behalf, leaving to the individual seller only the decision how much to offer at the agreed price. If the result is to induce a concentration of buying power on the other side, the two negotiating bodies must then take into account the estimated supply and demand curves for their product as a whole; the price obtainable for the quantity the producers wish to offer is set ultimately by the demand of the final consumers, transmuted through the costs and bargaining power of the processing trade. This trend towards bilateral bargaining was strongly re-inforced during the inter-war years, for reasons which are discussed later; the Hops Marketing Board, the Milk Marketing Boards and the Pigs Marketing Board all undertook between 1932 and 1939 the negotiation of annual contracts for the sale of their members' products. They then became the target for criticism for failing to obtain expanding markets at enhanced prices, for failing in fact to achieve the impossible. Whether contracts are negotiated collectively or individually, the secure market for the stated quantity usually implies a greater degree of variability and of insecurity for the quantity produced in excess of that which can be sold at the agreed price in the main market. The Hops Marketing Board has both restricted output by quota and also destroyed hops which could not be sold at the agreed price; the Milk Marketing Boards dispose of their surplus milk by sale for manufacture into various products at much lower prices than those obtainable in the liquid market.

IV. PRODUCE MARKETS

The organised produce market fulfills two main functions, firstly, the aggregation of demand and supply for the greater convenience of buyers and sellers, who thus obtain a higher degree of competition; secondly, the minimising of risk-taking over long distances or long periods of time through a high degree of specialisation of function. This division of risks is most important with fairly non-perishable products such as grain, oilseeds, tea, coffee, or rubber.

In its simplest form the produce market consists of a centre well served by transport and communication in which buyers and sellers can meet at pre-arranged times. Ungraded and perishable products such as fish, fruit and some vegetables, must also be physically present for inspection and immediate sale; more durable products, capable of being graded, can be sold by sample or description only. The advantages of such a market are those of (almost) perfect competition among experts who are in close touch both with consumer demand on the one hand and on the other with all the various sources of supply for the different grades and qualities. Yarn spinners can buy at the Bradford Wool Sales bulk lots of the particular wools required for their particular trade; greengrocers can buy at Covent Garden every variety of produce in an hour and are saved the costs of several dozen orders to several dozen different growers; livestock auctions serve both the local retail butcher, buying his meat 'on the hoof' and the wholesale meat traders re-selling at Smithfield to the multiple butchers who buy only the quality of meat required by their own localities. It is by such economies that produce markets justify the extra costs incurred when the commodities for sale have to be brought physically into the market, and out of it again.

From the producers' side, the advantages to be secured from these markets depend firstly on the economy of bulk transport and secondly on the proper presentation of their produce to the potential buyers. Much of the cost of modern transport consists in the identification, booking and handling of each consignment; a full wagon or lorry load is far cheaper to handle than the same volume made up of fifty different consignments, loaded and unloaded at different places and all requiring separate invoices, bills and receipts. Hence the local produce merchant in rural areas who buys locally and arranges bulk transport for potatoes or sprouts or celery from his district to the urban markets in London, Birmingham or Glasgow. Such merchants may buy outright, taking the risks of the market; or they may operate on a commission paid either by the growers or by the wholesale merchants. Only a large grower can usually deal direct both with the transport agency and with merchants in the produce market.

In such centres, grading and packing played an important part up to 1939 and that importance has again revived since the gradual improvement in food supplies after the end of the second world war. The good quality product, cleanly and clearly packed after proper selection and grading, usually meets with a demand sufficient to cover the extra cost; it is the poor quality product for which demand is apt to prove inelastic and price to fall heavily at any time when total supplies are temporarily excessive. This well-known phenomenon lies behind the claims for compulsory grading and for some control of total supply (as by a producers' marketing board) in the interests of the better quality products. It is the accurate grading and uniformity of imported foods which often gives them a substantial price differential over the British products, which come to market in small lots, usually ungraded and of very varying quality; the imported product can often be sold by sample or description only, while the home-grown produce has to be physically inspected, with all the extra costs of bringing it into and out of the central markets.

V. CO-OPERATIVE SOCIETIES

The essence of the co-operative society is three-fold; its control by its members who each have one vote only; the limitation of the return on its share capital, all provided by members; and the distribution of profits in proportion to the volume of each member's trade through the society. The early and fluctuating history of the agricultural co-operative movement in this country is outside the scope of this book;[1] but the societies now conduct a considerable volume of trade in farm supplies and claimed in 1954 a total membership of some 250,000; the exact number is presumably less than this since some farmers belonged to more than one society. The existing societies are the survivors of a considerably greater number not all of which lived to grow up, for the complexity of the marketing process and the great price falls of the inter-war years defeated many groups in their early days. The farmer-members were often slow to appreciate, and to pay, the value of a good manager and many societies failed to obtain a sufficient turnover to justify the overhead costs. Most of those that struggled

[1] M. Digby and S. Gorst, *Agricultural Co-operatives in the United Kingdom* (Blackwell, 1957).

through their teething troubles concentrated on the bulking of orders for the fairly standardised products required by farmers; a smaller number packed and graded fruit, vegetables, eggs or table poultry for their members to be sold in the large units favoured by the urban markets. It is noteworthy that farmers' co-operatives have had the greatest success in this country in areas with many family farms or market gardens of equal social status, areas such as Wales or the market gardens round Evesham.

In other countries less adequately equipped with distributive trades, the development of co-operative societies has been an essential part in the growth of a commercialised agriculture. They have played a large part in the Irish dairy industry, and indeed in the social life of the Irish countryside; farmers in New Zealand, Australia and Denmark have used co-operation in the development from small beginnings of their foreign trade in agricultural products. Where commercial experience and credit were both lacking, only the combined resources of a group of farmers could overcome the initial difficulties of a new trade and the risks of opening up new and distant markets.

VI. THE PROMOTION OF COMPETITION

The main effect in Britain of the agricultural co-operatives has probably been to stimulate and improve the degree of competition in the trades and localities in which they engage; they have provided another useful function in educating their members to appreciate the complexity of the marketing process and the economies to be secured by bulk purchase or sale. In a similar way, the Potato Marketing Board, from 1933 to 1939 and again after 1954, attempted to improve competition in local markets by providing information on trends and prices in central markets and also in buying potatoes itself if farmers could not find buyers at the current price. On the other hand, the Wool Marketing Board has suppressed competition between farmers by becoming the sole seller of home-grown wool; but it claims to have improved the competitive position of this product in international markets by better sorting and grading and by improved facilities for buyers. The Fatstock Marketing

Corporation was another attempt to improve competition in the markets in which farmers sell their fatstock. After the end of meat rationing in July 1954 the three National Farmers' Unions set up the Corporation to buy fatstock for re-sale as dead meat in wholesale markets or on contract to bacon factories; its activities have therefore supplemented those of the established traders whose operations, it was feared, after fourteen years of rationing and price control, might not be sufficiently competitive in some of the smaller markets. But it is important to realise in what circumstances such action to improve competition is likely to bring about greater efficiency or reduced marketing costs.

In conditions of imperfect competition, it is not possible to compel a firm, or a farmer, to behave as though competition was perfect. Let us suppose, by way of illustration, that we have in an area one processor, buying from farmers and selling to consumers in highly imperfect markets (Table 10). He may find that if he buys more than a stated quantity, the price he has to pay for all his purchases rises sharply against him; or if he tries to sell more than the usual quantity, the retail price falls. For any amount above these quantities, therefore, his marginal cost rises and his marginal revenue falls.

Table 10. *Marginal revenue to a merchant*

Units	Buying price	Total cost	Selling price	Total receipts	Total profit	Marginal revenue
80	13¾	1,100	21¼	1,700	600	–
90	14	1,260	21	1,890	630	+30
100	14½	1,450	20½	2,050	600	−30
110	15	1,650	19½	2,145	495	−105

In markets such as this, it does not pay this firm to buy more than 90 units; for any larger amount, its profits fall and there will presumably be a still greater fall in net profits after deduction of trading costs. If the trade could be more economically carried out by 10 firms each processing 9 or 10 units and trading in fully competitive markets, then it is possible that about 100 units would be bought at a wholesale price of 14½ and sold at about 20½. But such a state of affairs is improbable; the smaller firms are likely in modern conditions to be less efficient processors than one large firm and their total costs would therefore be higher; they could not all survive in the trade; they would either diminish in numbers or agree among themselves not to compete in a reduction of margins below those required to keep them all comfortably in business. In these latter circumstances, when a trade has become fossilised into conventional margins, the introduction of a strong competitor, backed with ample funds to meet initial costs and risks, may well improve competition and reduce distributive margins; but in the process some existing firms will be forced out of business and the reduction in numbers will again diminish the force of competition and increase the possibility of monopolistic influences.

This conflict between efficiency, in the sense of lowest total costs, and the maintenance of competition as a guarantee against monopoly profits may be illustrated from the history of the milk market.[1] Farmers selling milk on wholesale contracts frequently complained between the wars of the semi-monopolistic power over prices, both wholesale and retail, which could be exercised by the half-dozen largest buyers for the urban milk markets; they claimed that the distributive margin provided more than adequate returns for the functions performed and that either wholesale prices should be higher or that retail prices should be lower, with consequently a larger market. A succession of official enquiries showed that a reduction in the almost conventional margins would immediately force out of business many of the producer-retailers operating on a small scale on the fringes of urban centres; their trade would be taken over by the large firms; there would be a rationalisation of rounds and a fall in costs; but such a process would reduce what competition there was and increase the power of the large firms. It was only during the war that the conflict between efficiency and competition was resolved in favour of the first; retail milk rounds were rationalised with a consequent reduction in distributive costs and the

[1] See reports of the Reorganisation Commission for Milk, 1933; 1935; of the (Perry) Committee on the Cost of Milk Distribution, 1940; of the (Williams) Committee on Milk Distribution, Cmd. 7414, 1948; E. Strauss, 'Structure of the English Milk Industry', *J.R.S.S.* (1960), vol. 123.

elimination of consumer choice. Since that date, both retail milk prices and the wholesale prices paid by the distributors have remained under State control; and there has been a steady fall in the number of producer-retailers operating.

In this particular case, the economies which could be achieved in transport and manpower by the consolidation of retail rounds were so large that, in the emergency of war, a cut in distributive margins could be enforced. It might be thought therefore that once competition in any trade has become conspicuously imperfect, the best remedy is centralised control over margins, setting at least upper limits. But experience during the war showed that this process has its own dangers and may itself lead to an appreciable rise in total costs, rather than a decrease. While there is any competition in a trade, some firms will be losing business and others will be expanding through greater efficiency. The costs of distribution include not only the profits of the latter but also the losses of the former and are therefore lower than might appear from contemplating only the successful firms. Further, the distributive trades normally work on fairly stable average margins over a period of time and over a variety of commodities. Fluctuating prices for the basic products are often offset against each other in order to avoid frequent changes in the quoted prices for the final products. If the retail demand for beef is elastic to a rise in price and inelastic to a fall in price from the current level, then butchers tend to keep retail prices unchanged and to accept a fluctuating margin in accordance with changes in wholesale prices over time; or when cattle are dear, the reduced margin is met from a higher margin on lamb. Distributors, like farmers, are concerned to make the best profit they can over their past expenditure; and their current sales policy must be related primarily to current demand. But margins fixed by State control, or by a process of collective bargaining between semi-monopolistic bodies, cannot take these fluctuations and balances into account, and may lead to major total costs than occur in trades retaining even a mild degree of competition. Unless there are large economies to be secured only by large units, unless competition has become virtually extinct and its revival involves dis-economies on a considerable scale, competition between farmers and firms alike is probably the best guarantee of a reasonable measure of efficiency.

VII. THE SUPPRESSION OF COMPETITION

Yet over the last twenty years competition in agricultural markets has become hardly respectable. The arguments in favour of more competition, commonly heard in the first thirty years of this century, gave way between the wars to pleas for limited supplies, stable markets, combined selling, control of 'cut-throat' competition and the like. Under the Agricultural Marketing Acts (1931, 1933, 1949), a two-thirds majority of growers of any agricultural product (controlling at least two-thirds of the output) can set up a Marketing Board as the sole seller of that product, able to regulate its terms of sale, the amount which can be sold and in some cases the production as well. The reasons for this change in the climate of opinion are both complex and important.

We noted earlier that there are certain trends in the process of economic development which may lead to a worsening of the terms of trade for agricultural products and a falling aggregate income for their suppliers. A rapid flow of technical improvements and a demand inelastic both to price and income changes can combine into a semi-permanent trend of weak markets and falling prices. Such a conjunction occurred most markedly from 1920 in most types of commercial agriculture. These long-term trends aggravated the instability of many agricultural markets under chance variations in supplies and encouraged experiments in 'stock-piling' as a remedy for periodic gluts, on the pattern discussed in the previous chapter. Then again, many farmers attributed their unfavourable prices during these years to the growth of monopolistic practices among the distributive trades or to 'unfair' competition from other groups of farmers who took advantage of falling costs in production and transport to explore new markets. The best remedy, it was often argued, was more monopoly, this time organised by the producers. Again the first world war and its financial consequences disrupted the old mechanism of international trade. For some years after the end of hostilities, foreign exchanges fluctuated wildly as unstable Governments grappled with inflation of their currencies; the general fall in prices from the peak in the spring of 1920 added to the financial troubles of traders and Governments alike. The return of Britain to the gold standard in 1925 undoubtedly brought greater stability to the financing of the international trade in agricultural products, but also brought a further measure of deflation in this country with renewed pressure on the prices of those products most exposed to foreign competition.

Finally the fall in the prices of agricultural products relative to those of industry was intensified after 1929 by the great depression originating in that year. The causes, course and effects of that depression have been endlessly discussed, since it left an indelible mark on the development and politics of all the major countries. But in this connection, we need only note that the depression was primarily a depression in industrial production and employment and in agricultural prices and incomes. Confronted by an unexpected and general fall in prices, large sections of industry shut down, putting plants out of operation and men out of employment and income; this fall in supply helped to maintain the price level of these products. The reaction of many farmers throughout the world was just the opposite; as prices fell they tended to work harder and to consume less so that supply increased; taken as a whole, the supply of agricultural products tended to be inelastic to a general fall in prices, and this intensified the fall in agricultural prices. In Britain, the fall in farm incomes was mitigated partly by the restriction on imports of competing foods, partly by an intricate system of subsidies; it was the countries exporting agricultural produce which suffered the greatest fall in agricultural income, since the partial closure of foreign markets intensified the price fall in their internal markets. Thus the total value of agricultural output is estimated to have fallen, between 1929 and 1932, in the United States from $11,900 m. to $5,142 m.; in New Zealand from £83 m. to £50 m.; and in Australia from £223 m. to £148 m.[1] Those who were farming

---

[1] League of Nations, *World Economic Survey, 1933-4*, p. 297. See also D. Gale Johnson, 'Supply of Agricultural Products', *American Economic Review* (Sept. 1950), pp. 539-64.

in these years found that prices which equated a falling demand with a constant supply were so low that a high proportion of farmers were bankrupt; since demand was outside their control, they turned to the restriction of supply as the principal remedy, a measure which itself involved the suppression of competition between growers of each product in favour of some central selling agency. In country after country during these years, there were established farmers' selling pools, agricultural marketing boards, State-authorised buying agencies, central export commissions, all charged with the main task of eliminating competition in primary markets, of controlling supplies, of fixing minimum prices to growers, and of administering State subsidies to distressed farmers.

As emergency measures to meet an overwhelming economic blizzard, these bodies played a minor part in temporarily holding prices, in checking the fall in farm incomes and in restoring confidence in panic-stricken markets. But once the worst of the storm was over, the enduring problems re-emerged. A price level which provided farmers with what they regarded as a 'reasonable' level of incomes would induce a volume of supply which could not possibly be sold at these prices and also a volume of criticism from the urban population, confronted with a rise in the cost of their basic foods at a time of heavy unemployment; control of supply to prevent the accumulation of unsold stocks was almost as unpopular with farmers as lower prices, since it struck not only at their incomes but also hindered the adaptation of production to technical progress. By the end of the decade, it was generally recognised that the suppression of competition along these lines could not do more than diminish the fluctuations in farm incomes; to raise them, both absolutely and in relation to other incomes, required a general rise in consumer demand for agricultural products or a radical change in the conditions of supply.

Both these requirements were met by war, for those farmers who were not directly in the battlefields. Shortage of supply, created by shortages of fertilisers, of machinery and of labour, was combined with rising demand from civilians with full employment and larger incomes, and from Governments catering for millions of men in uniform. But food shortages on the scale induced by total war brought also food rationing, price control and centralised buying by many Governments. In war-time, the satisfaction of consumer demand ceases to be the main object of production and free market prices cannot therefore be allowed to determine the use of resources; consumers must be fed with the minimum use of scarce factors at the lowest standards that they can be induced to tolerate. The State control over the production and distribution of food indirectly favoured the proliferation of negotiating bodies in all the trades affected—selling organisations among farmers and overseas suppliers, trade committees of importers, wholesalers, processors and retailers to bargain over margins and to organise the detail of control. Because rising prices and satisfactory profits earned during the war were associated with rigid control of markets, competition seems to have become linked, in the minds of many farmers, with the falling prices and financial distress of the inter-war years and therefore to be regarded as totally undesirable, or even immoral.

The analysis of the preceding chapters has shown that such an association, however plausible, cannot be correct; changes in the structure of marketing, reform or revolution in the distributive trades cannot substantially affect the long-term trends in supply and demand which determine the relative income levels of the urban and farm populations. But the peculiarities of agricultural supply, to some extent, justify a semi-monopolistic seller who can prevent periodic gluts from reaching the markets and thus mitigate, to some extent, the drastic falls in price which accompany them. Again, if competition in wholesale markets becomes overlaid by restrictive tendencies, or dies naturally through the economies of large-scale processing or transport, then a case can be made either for collective action by the primary sellers or for some supervision by the State. And thirdly, State intervention to alter the distribution of income resulting from market prices can often be most economical when exercised in conjunction with a central agency representing the producers.

Since 1950, farmers in the United Kingdom have established (by majority votes) the Wool Marketing Board, a Tomato and Cucumber Marketing Board and an Egg Marketing Board;

the Potato Marketing Board has been revived; the Milk Marketing Boards have been restored to their pre-war status, shorn only of their powers to determine wholesale and retail prices for liquid milk. But a marketing scheme proposed for apples and pears was rejected by small majorities of the growers concerned; it has also been agreed not to revive the triple structure of Pigs Marketing Board, Bacon Marketing Board and Bacon Development Board which functioned from 1933 to 1936, but to rely instead on a price guarantee scheme, operated by the State, to minimise price fluctuations. These post-war developments are described later; our next step is to look at the conditions of agricultural supply which have been responsible, jointly with the conditions of demand, for the relatively low levels of agricultural incomes.

Further Reading

The Ministry of Agriculture and Fisheries published between 1920 and 1947 a number of reports on the marketing of agricultural products—the Economic Series, 1-48.

For the post-war period, see

Report of the (Lucas) Committee on the Agricultural Marketing Schemes (1947).
Report of the (Williams) Committee on Milk Distribution (Cmd. 7414, 1948).
Report of the (Bosanquet) Reorganisation Commission for Pigs and Bacon (Cmd. 9795, 1956).
Report of the (Runciman) Committee on Horticultural Marketing (Cmnd. 61,1957).
Report on the Agricultural Marketing Schemes, 1938-1955 (Cmnd. 57, 1957).
Report on the Proposed British Egg Marketing Scheme (Cmd. 9805, 1958).
L. G. Bennett, *The Marketing of Horticultural Produce Grown in Bedfordshire, West Cornwall, Wisbech and the Lea Valley.* Reading Department of Agricultural Economics, Miscellaneous Studies No. 12 (1957).
L. G. Bennett, *The Wholesale Trade in Horticultural Produce in Smithfield Market, Birmingham.* Reading, Department of Agricultural Economics, Miscellaneous Studies No. 13 (1957).
R. J. Hammond, *Food*, vol. 1 'The Growth of Policy' (H.M.S.O. and Longmans, 1951).
E. A. Attwood and G. Hallett, 'Marketing of Farm Products in the U.K.' *J.R.A.S.* (1958), vol. 119 pp. 19-33.

CHAPTER V

THE SUPPLY OF AGRICULTURAL PRODUCE

The main characteristic of modern farming as part of the national economy is the very large number of separate units each in a small way of business; in this it resembles the pattern of retail distribution, as distinct from the much larger units in which manufacturing industry is usually organised. This large number of independent units exists because of two other characteristics of agriculture, its extension over space and its dependence on biological and climatic factors.

I. THE NUMBER OF HOLDINGS IN BRITAIN

In Great Britain the number of agricultural holdings has remained remarkably stable over the seventy years for which statistics are available. If the holdings under 5 acres are ignored as being not commercial farms in the usual sense (though some may be market gardens), it appears that more than half of the British holdings are less than 50 acres in size,

Table 11. *Number of agricultural holdings in Great Britain, 1931, 1951, 1956*

Size group (acres)	1931	1951 (thousands)	1956
5–15	213·4	91·4	86·4
15–49		100·3	95·5
50–99	72·2	70·0	68·9
100–149	37·9	36·9	36·4
150–299	41·7	40·0	39·7
above 300	14·5	14·8	15·4
	379·7	353·4	342·3

Source: Agricultural Statistics, 1939, 1956/7.

and only 16 per cent exceed 150 acres (Table 11). Two qualifications must be noted in making deductions from these statistics. A farmer who combines two holdings under one management may continue to supply two returns until the recording authority somehow becomes aware of the change, so that the number of holdings is always larger than the number of separate businesses. Secondly, war-time administration brought into the returns a considerable number of the smaller holdings which had previously been omitted, so that the fall in numbers between 1931 and 1951 was rather larger than that actually recorded. Allowing for these uncertainties, it is still true that there has been surprisingly little change in the size distribution of holdings, in spite of wars and technical changes in the practice of farming. And this stability is confirmed by a corresponding stability in the numbers of persons returned as farmers in the decennial census. Such changes as are shown in Table 12 seem to reflect small changes in the census schedules rather than economic trends. Why is the family farm so stable a unit in agriculture when in industry limited liability companies employing tens or hundreds of people is the norm?

Table 12. *Number of farmers in Great Britain, 1851, 1911, 1931, 1951*

1851	1911	1931	1951
303,000	279,000	294,000	302,000

Source: J. R. Bellerby, 'Distribution of Manpower in Agriculture and Industry, 1851–1951', *Farm Economist*, vol. IX (1958), No. 1, pp. 1–11.

The extension of farming over space is an obvious difficulty to the growth of large units in agriculture. Details of management require transport and time, both of them costly; the larger the unit, the greater the proportion of time that will be spent in travel and the greater the chance that something will go wrong for want of the farmer's presence. Nor does the amalgamation of two farms always provide an economic unit for operation. Unless they are contiguous, transport and time may be required in their management on a prohibitive scale; even if the two units adjoin, their roads, buildings, fields and water supplies cannot easily be adapted for common working from a convenient centre. The pressure to expand the business has in fact resulted in many disjointed holdings in this country, farms run in conjunction with a couple of grazing fields in the next parish, or even small blocks of land separated not only from each other but also from the farm house and buildings. Expansion in this way, by acquiring disconnected pieces of land as they become available, clearly adds to the difficulties of management and is unlikely to proceed far. Save in a few countries, it is no longer possible for the area of cultivated land to be appreciably increased without substantial investment in irrigation, drainage or pest control. An industrialist can build another and larger factory, but before a farmer can expand his farm, he has to acquire some other farmer's land. The total area of land is fixed within narrow limits in a manner which does not apply to factories or shops.

The dependence of farming on biological and climatic factors prohibits any regular routine in farming operations. A farmer may be singling beet on Monday, sheep shearing on Tuesday, cutting hay on Wednesday, cleaning the combine while the rain falls on Thursday, making silage on Friday, taking the pigs to market on Saturday, and wrestling with accounts on Sunday. Each of the week-day operations involves a separate decision on the condition of the crop or the animals, the effect of yesterday's weather and the current prospects, the combination of men and machinery in appropriate units, the relative cost of not doing a job now because the weather is unsuitable and of doing it next week when the weather may be better but the crop or animal in a less suitable stage or the labour force likely to be busier. Indeed, almost the only routine job on most British farms is that of milking, performed twice a day seven days a week, Sundays and Bank Holidays included, but growing fodder for the cows and rearing their replacements cannot be so simply standardised. Because there is so little routine, management cannot easily be either standardised or delegated. It is indeed a criticism sometimes made of the mixed farming found in this country that on a large scale its managerial problems are too complicated for any but the most outstanding men to attain a high degree of all-round efficiency. Motor transport, the telephone, cost accounting, have in the last fifty years eased the task of the manager of a large farm but the barrier has not been abolished, only moved a little further off.

II. THE STRUCTURE OF FARM COSTS

All these factors combine to make the physical extension of a farm costly and difficult, while above a certain size there is little scope for economies of large-scale output and many possibilities of waste. Nor can farmers indefinitely intensify their output from a given area; as we noted on p. 18, if we assume average management and no changes in technique, we have one of the oldest of economic generalisations, that the application of successive units of any factors to a fixed quantity of one factor will, after a point, produce diminishing returns. If we convert this expression from physical quantities to money values we can say that, with constant technique and after a certain point, the cost of obtaining successive units of output from a given area of land will inevitably increase Table 13. With this pattern, the scale of output is determined by the point at which marginal cost is equal to the price obtained in the market for the product, but the average cost may be substantially below the price received, and it is from this difference

Table 13. *Marginal cost*

Units sold	Total cost	Average cost per unit	Marginal cost
7	70	10	—
8	80	10	10
9	99	11	19
10	120	12	21
11	143	13	23

that the farmer draws his own income. The relationship between average cost and price decides whether or not a farmer stays in the business at all, while the relationship of marginal cost to price determines the level of his most profitable output in current conditions. Hence we find a very wide range of average costs for any of the major farm products, yet the farm with low average costs may not be able to expand without adding more to its costs than to its receipts; when adjusted to the current level of costs and prices, each farm should have attained its most profitable output, with marginal costs about equal to the price obtained.

In this highly simplified analysis, it has been assumed that each farm produces only one product, an assumption which is near enough the truth for Australian wheat farmers or New Zealand dairy farmers, but which is wide of the mark for most farms in Britain. For the mixed crops-and-livestock farm, it is clear that average and marginal costs as defined above include different items. From any given output, the marginal cost is the extra cost of producing one more unit, or the expenditure that will be saved by producing one unit less. We are here dealing only with those costs that change with small changes in output—expenditure on fertilisers, or seeds, or feeding-stuffs, or casual labour, or tractor fuel. In deciding whether it pays to add one more cow to his herd, a farmer would not need to consider the regular wage paid to his cowman, or his own living expenses or the depreciation of his milking plant or tractor. For this particular decision, these costs are fixed; the farmer has to pay them whether he has 19 cows or 20. But his average costs per gallon of milk must include all costs directly attributable to his dairy herd—the upkeep of his milking plant as well as the wages and insurance of his cowman, a payment for the farmers' own time and that part of his tractor costs which is directly incurred in producing and moving fodder for his cows. And many accountants would also include in average costs an allowance for part of the general overhead expenses of the farm—the rent or the interest payable on the mortgage, the upkeep of buildings, the maintenance work on hedges and ditches, the farm car and the farm telephone. It has been calculated, for instance, that on the small, mainly dairy, farms of Northern Ireland about one-third of total costs can strictly be allocated to the production of individual commodities;[1] a substantial proportion even of these might not be affected by small changes in output.

This high proportion of overhead costs has four practical results. Firstly, the calculation of average costs of production for any farm product involves a large element of arbitrary allocation

[1] V. Liversage, 'Farm Costs', *J.A.E.*, vol. IX No. 1, (1950), pp. 54-63.

of costs which are incurred jointly in the production of several saleable commodities. A comparison of average costs between farms is therefore dangerous unless the farms are of roughly similar type and the same methods of cost accounting have been used for all of them.

Secondly, in deciding what scale of output is most profitable, farmers following a mixed pattern take into account only a narrow range of costs. Their argument runs: if I produce one unit more of A and one unit less of B, what is likely to be the effect firstly on my expenditure and secondly on my receipts? The costs reckoned for this decision are only those which change with changes in the scale of output, and they may be quite a small proportion of the total costs. Hence from a mixed farming system, the output of individual commodities is liable to quite substantial changes with small changes in relative profitability between different enterprises, since only a narrow range of costs are considered against the yields and prices of the different products.

Thirdly, the farmer who employs only himself and perhaps a member of his family full or part time, has clearly a very high proportion of joint and unallocated costs; he will not normally cost his own time, in reckoning whether an increase in output is worth while; a change will be worth making if it brings in any surplus over his extra *money* costs, and the lower his income, the more valuable to him the extra income in relation to any extra work involved. If output has not been accurately adjusted to the current level of prices, a fall in those prices may induce such farmers, paradoxically, to offset the fall in income by working more, consuming less and thus temporarily selling a larger supply. Thus during the general fall in prices from 1929 to 1932, agricultural output in many countries tended to rise rather than to fall.

Fourthly, and more important than this temporary pheno- menon, is the strong pressure on all farms, with their limited area and high proportion of overhead costs, to adopt every technical improvement which is likely to increase output without raising costs or requiring much additional capital. The better educated are the farmers, the more closely they are in touch with scientists and engineers, the more rapidly technical improvements will be adopted, and the stronger the general trend towards an increase in the supply from each farm. Arthur Young commented early in the nineteenth century that improvements travelled at the rate of a mile a year; that would be faster progress than can be obtained in many primitive communities, dominated by custom, ignorance, limited markets and communal land tenures. But a commercialised agriculture serving an industrial and scientific community which provides a high level of general education can expect from its farms a rapid rate of technical progress, as each farmer tries to raise his income by spreading his overhead costs over a steadily increasing output. The increasing costs which prevent a society at a low level of technique from expanding its food supply are converted, under the influence of science, technology and education, to a flow of improvements which enable farmers to increase supply at falling real costs, to obtain an increasing output per unit of combined input. And it is this increase in supply, combined with a low income-elasticity of demand for many agricultural products, which in turn produces the effects noted earlier, the falling price level for agricultural products relative to those for industrial products.

III. THE ELASTICITY OF SUPPLY
FOR ALL AGRICULTURAL PRODUCTS

To a considerable extent, therefore, the supply of agricultural produce, taken as a whole, does not in a modern society respond to price changes, whether up or down; over a period of years, it continues to expand by a momentum of its own, derived partly from technical progress and partly from the structure of farming, with the large number of family businesses each restricted to a certain area of land. It has been calculated that, over the forty years from 1910 to 1950, the output from agriculture in the United States increased by 75 per cent or by about 2 per cent per annum.[1] Of this total increase, about half was ascribed to greater efficiency in production and about half to a greater supply of inputs whose composition greatly changed

[1] T. W. Schultz, 'Contribution of the Economist to Programmes of Technical Development, I.C.A.E. (1955), p. 475.

over these forty years. A similar trend is apparent for products derived from highly specialised farms which cannot easily turn from one product to another, wheat from Australia or dairying in New Zealand and Britain. It has been shown that price changes have little influence on the output of butter fat from New Zealand dairy farms.[1] The continued expansion in their output is derived from the pressure to raise their income by obtaining greater receipts from their limited land and family labour; the variations in this upward trend have been the result, not of planned responses to profit changes, but of the variability of the season, since the cows live almost entirely from pasture all the year round. The same seems also to hold for the output of milk from dairy farms in the United Kingdom, a product especially favoured by the large numbers of family farms.

For all agricultural products taken together, therefore, and for products from specialised farms, we cannot justly use the concept of a 'supply curve', such as we drew in Chapter III. At almost any level of profit, supply will tend to expand; the 'supply curve' becomes an almost vertical line shifting year by year to the right, implying that, other things being equal, there will be a larger supply in each successive year over any usual range of price. Recent experience has also shown that this expansion in supply is likely to be greater if agricultural incomes are high than if they are low, relative to other earnings. Both in the United States and the United Kingdom, aggregate output expanded slowly during the years between the wars, when aggregate agricultural incomes were either falling or nearly stationary; in both countries there was a rapid expansion during the war when agricultural incomes increased both absolutely and in relation to other incomes; and the trend continued into the post-war years. Our 'supply curve' for agricultural products in industrialised communities may be visualised as a series of parallel lines, indicating that whatever the level of prices, output will increase from year 1 to year 2 and year 3, but the increase will be greater at high prices than at low prices.

But it would be rash indeed to estimate the probable future

[1] R. W. M. Johnson, 'Aggregate Supply of New Zealand Farm Products,' *Economic Record*, vol. xxxi (1955), pp. 50–60.

degree of elasticity of supply for all agricultural products in general from past experience, since the rate of expansion depends not only on prices but also very largely on the technical improvements open at any time to the majority of farmers concerned; these cannot be the same in the future as in the past decade. We must admit, therefore, that a 'supply curve' for agricultural products taken as a whole is a highly abstract concept for the aggregation of output from hundreds of thousands of farmers, each re-acting in his own way to changes in the opportunities for making profits, whether those changes arise from changes in prices or from changes in possible techniques.

IV. THE ELASTICITY OF SUPPLY FOR ONE PRODUCT

A supply curve for any individual product can perhaps be more closely related to the actual world of farms and farmers. We are considering here the re-action of farmers to actual or expected changes in the profits to be made from the production and sale of one commodity, out of the many commonly produced on the mixed farms found in Britain and in parts of the United States. In strict theory, we must assume that all other things remain unchanged, though clearly, in practice, we must allow for the existing trend in the output of that commodity and for the technical improvements which are known and capable of adoption by the ordinary farmer. Within these trends, it must also be recognised that soil, altitude and climate between them often set more or less definite limits to the physical area over which any one product or group of allied products can be grown. In Britain, differences in annual rainfall distinguish broadly the mainly arable regions found in the south and east, from the mainly grassland regions of the west and north. Changes in the relative profits derived from livestock and arable shift the balance between these two types of farming to and fro across the 35–40 inch rain contour, running roughly from the Exe to Teeside and northward to include a narrow belt of coastal land up to the Moray Firth. West of this line, the greater rainfall hinders harvesting, lowers crop yields and therefore raises the cost of growing grain and root crops, while it encourages the more even growth of grass throughout the season. Again, steep slopes, thin soils over rocks, high rainfall and severe winds make arable cultivation impossible in this country on most land over 800–1,000 feet; the extent to which cultivation can be pushed up the slopes is largely determined by economic factors of prices and costs, the latter reflecting the technical efficiency of men in devising tools and power. And in continental regions, the cost of transport to consuming centres has exercised a strong influence on land use, an influence which has diminished as transport by water, rail, road and air has progressively cheapened and quickened the movement of goods and persons over space. The structure of land use, the division of the available area between forestry, pasture, cultivated grass and arable crops thus reflects the basic facts of physical geography; but the immediate pattern is set within this structure by the influence of the relative prices and costs of agricultural products.

The reaction of farmers to relative price changes are conditioned firstly by the extent of joint products and of joint costs; secondly by the risk and uncertainty attached to price changes; and thirdly by the availability of the factors of production, a matter which deserves the next chapter to itself.

In England and Wales, wheat and barley are grown throughout the eastern and southern counties in a common crop rotation. For optimum growth they require rather different conditions of soil and climate, but the specific costs attributable to each in the rotation are small; moreover, up to a point, they are competitive crops. Hence, quite a small change in the relative profitability of wheat and barley will result in a large shift in area, as was demonstrated after 1932 when the Wheat Act provided a guaranteed price that could not diverge far from 10s. per cwt. (Table 14).[1]

It must be remembered that these changes took place from a comparatively low level of area grown; the elasticity of supply here indicated could not reasonably be expected from such areas as were attained in 1944 and 1945, when the production

[1] T. W. Gardner, 'Cereal Prices and Acreages', *J.A.E.*, vol. xii, No. 3 (1957), pp. 361–70.

Table 14. *Elasticity of supply of wheat in England and Wales, 1929–37*

	Wheat			Barley	
	Thousand acres	Price per cwt.		Thousand acres	Price per cwt.
		s.	d.		s.	d.
1929	1,330	9	2	1,120	9	3
1930	1,346	6	1	1,020	8	11
1931	1,197	6	1	1,029	8	10
1932	1,288	9	10†	961	7	6
1933	1,660	9	6	751	9	9
1934	1,759	8	8½	861	9	0
1935	1,772	9	1½	792	8	10
1936	1,704	9	10½	819	10	1
1937	1,732	9	11½	823	12	9

Area in June; price for harvest year beginning in year given.
† Including deficiency payments in this and later years.
Source: Agricultural Statistics.

of both crops was being pushed almost to the physical limits. Sugar beet and potatoes present similar features of joint costs with other crops in the rotation, and also compete with each other in areas near sugar beet factories.

In contrast to these pairs of competing products with a high proportion of joint costs, a shift from beef production to a dairy herd, or from arable cropping to fruit trees, involves a radical change in the farming enterprise. Such changes are unlikely to be made unless there is a fairly large shift in the balance of profitability and only after a considerable time lag. And the more specialised the farm, the fewer the products it sells, the less scope it has for changing the pattern of output to meet minor changes in profitability. A community of mixed farms each producing milk with a variety of other livestock products and some crops, may show a fairly high elasticity in response to changes in product prices; a community of wheat farms or cattle ranches or sheep runs may stagnate for years while other types of farming rake in the money. Hence the agricultural economist must understand the technical and economic factors conditioning the output of any product before he can make reasonable forecasts of its elasticity of supply.[1]

[1] F. Holmes, 'Estimating a Supply Curve', *J.A.E.*, vol. XIII, No. 1 (1958), pp. 67–71.

V. UNCERTAINTY

The time taken before changes in supply become effective is closely connected with the degree of uncertainty which afflicts prices. There are three sources of uncertainty which farmers face in deciding on their production plans. There is the uncertainty which results from ignorance of the current facts, the production plans of other farmers, the seasonal variations in demand, the trend in market prices. There is the uncertainty of the immediate future, over which there can only be estimates of the probability of certain trends developing—the size of next year's harvest and its effect on the prices of grain or vegetables, the changes in consumer demand for milk or beef, the prospects of alternative sources of supply. Thirdly, there is the varying risk undertaken by each farmer in framing and executing his production plan—the extent to which his financial status will be affected if a large commitment to a market turns out unfavourably, the extent to which it is worth risking a serious loss in the hope of a substantial gain. The longer the interval between a change in production plans and the consequent change in sales, the greater the financial investment involved, the greater becomes the risk of a severe financial loss which the established farmer may be able to carry but which may break the young man or the farmer on the margin of profitability.

In the first example given above, we are comparing the effect on production, as measured by area grown, of a known and guaranteed price for wheat against a variable and unknown price for barley, at a time when all agricultural prices and incomes were at their lowest point of the great depression. The marginal costs of growing rather more wheat and rather less barley are negligible on most farms, though there are differences in yields and therefore in returns per acre on different soils. A known price for wheat guaranteed for some years ahead is likely in such circumstances to result in a strong reaction in output; farmers on the edge of bankruptcy will grow wheat on land whose expected yield in a normal year will provide, at the guaranteed price, total receipts greater than their known money costs. When in financial straits, many farmers rightly prefer the known profit, even if small, to the chance of obtaining something bigger which yet may involve them in financial loss if the market falls still lower. The absence of risk in such circumstances will attract a much larger increase in supply than would probably occur if farming generally was in a prosperous condition.

Even in normal times there are so many reasons why market prices fluctuate that farmers are naturally slow to react to a recently established differential of uncertain duration. We looked at some of these reasons in Chapter III. There are the unplanned variations in yields; the exaggerated effect on prices of a derived demand acting in expectation of a further change; the long-term changes in demand as tastes and incomes alter; the frequent changes in demand induced by changes in other markets, such as the effect on sales of butter of price changes for margarine the changes in supply created by technical developments whose final results are often unpredictable in the early stages; the effects on individual markets of the ebb and flow of cyclical changes in the general price level.

Before a farmer changes his production plans, he should, in theory, have sufficient knowledge of current trends to make a reasoned judgment of the cause of a price change, of its probable duration and of the probable reaction of all his fellow-farmers and potential competitors. He must consider whether the production requires much capital or special skill which, once invested, may be useless if the market again becomes unfavourable; he must consider the length of the production period in relation to the duration of the price change. With this intense complexity, it is not surprising that farmers' responses to price changes are sometimes mistaken, as has been shown, for instance, to be the case for potatoes and other vegetables. Some lessening of price fluctuations was achieved by the Potato Marketing Board between 1933 and 1939 and again after 1954, but other vegetables are too variable in quality and too perishable for similar measures to be feasible.[1]

A striking case of self-perpetuating fluctuations was the inter-war cycle in pig numbers in almost all countries where pigs are fed on cereals. When pig prices were high and grain

[1] See above, p. 35.

prices low, it was reasonable to plan for an expanded pig herd, but two elements of uncertainty existed—the effect of another harvest, possibly a bad one, on grain prices, and the effect on future pig markets of the aggregate change in production plans by all other farmers. Because pig production has a short production period, need not involve much capital investment, and need not disrupt the long-term plans of a mixed farm, production changes tended to be greater in the aggregate than would probably be indicated by a rational calculation based on complete knowledge of all intentions.

For commodities such as pigs and vegetables, the changes in market prices required to equate demand with immediately available supply thus tend to produce changes in production plans which may themselves add to the irrationality of price movements; supply responds too easily and too much to price changes, however induced. On the other hand, where more radical changes in the internal structure of farms is concerned, elasticity of supply is likely to be low and late to develop, as for instance between grain crops as an aggregate and livestock products as another group. There is indeed a margin within which many farmers in the United Kingdom can shift fairly easily between grain and temporary grass or kale; but mainly arable farmers will not abandon grain growing and mainly stock farmers in the west and midlands will not grow larger areas of grain unless there is a large balance of advantage and one thought likely to be of some duration.

In somewhat the same category come those products whose output requires considerable capital investment in specialised equipment—hops, or orchards, or milk for the liquid market. Farmers will not risk their capital, especially if it is borrowed, on such equipment without a strong probability that their investment will, over a considerable period, bring a greater return than less risky enterprises. Conversely, once such investment has been made, the new level of supply is likely to continue as long as the returns cover the operating money costs, or until the original equipment becomes worn out. For such products, fluctuations in demand may result in large changes in profits, in conspicuous alterations between high prices and scarcity and low prices and excess supply; the elasticity of supply will be very low in the short period, both for a rise in profits and for a fall.

The elasticity of supply in response to price changes is thus a deceptively simple phrase concealing the vast complexities of modern production. In an industrialised society with well-organised scientific and advisory services, agricultural output taken as a whole has developed a long-term upward trend, intermittently stronger for some products than for others, but likely to persist at almost any level of farming profits. In addition, products with a short production period and requiring little capital investment may show too high an elasticity, in the sense that chance variations in prices give rise to an excessive variation in supply which again reacts on to prices. The supply of other products may react only sluggishly to price changes, because there is a long interval between a change in production plans and a change in sales, or because large capital investment is required, or because the current capital equipment has a long life before it wears out, or because farmers do not always bother to ascertain just what prices have changed. Almost 70 per cent of pig producers visited by one enquirer in June 1957 had not heard of the revised system of guaranteed pig prices announced and bought into force three months previously.[1] The response of farmers to varying degrees of risk and uncertainty is itself unpredictable, since it depends on recent experience of the markets, on current levels of income, on the urgency with which extra income is sought or losses avoided, and finally on the available supplies and costs of all the many things which farmers need. We must take a brief look at these markets before we leave the problems of agricultural supply.

[1] D. S. Thornton, 'Influence of the Annual Price Reviews on Pig Producers' Decisions', *J.A.E.*, vol. XIII, No. 2 (1958), pp. 192–7.

Further Reading

E. O. Heady, *Economics of Agricultural Production and Resource Use* (New York, 1952).

F. Holmes, 'Estimating a Supply Curve', *J.A.E.*, vol. XIII, No. 1 (1958), pp. 67–71.

G. R. Allen, 'Short-Term Production Variations for Horticultural Products and the Marketing System', *Farm Economist*, vol. VIII, No. 6 (1956), pp. 1–27.

G. R. Allen, *Agricultural Marketing Policies* (Blackwell, 1959).

F. G. Sturrock, *Farm Accounting and Management.* 3rd edition (Pitman, 1950).

CHAPTER VI

THE SUPPLY OF LAND AND CAPITAL

Technical efficiency requires the constant adaptation of inputs to meet changes in techniques of production and in the costs of the various factors. With a given pattern and a given level of output, costs will be least when each of the many requirements is employed in that quantity (1) for which the marginal cost is roughly equal to the value of the marginal product; (2) which gives returns for the last £10 spent on it roughly equal to those given by each of the other factors for the same cost. It is only worth while spending £10 on hiring another acre of land if gross receipts will be increased by more than £10; and if £10 spent on land adds more to receipts than the same sum spent on fertilisers or labour. The amount which a farmer should buy of each of these factors therefore depends firstly on its technical efficiency in production on his farm; secondly on its price; and thirdly on its availability. For the ideal combination of inputs to give lowest costs is in practice restricted firstly by the lumpiness of some of the factors, their lack of divisibility into small units; and secondly by discontinuities in supply to individual farmers. These imperfections in the combination of factors of production cause many of the peculiarities in the supply of agricultural products discussed in the last chapter.

I. THE SUPPLY OF LAND IN TOTAL

If we take the supply of land as fixed by natural causes; if we have an agriculture with a stable technique which operates under increasing costs; then the price of land (whether expressed in rent or sale value) depends primarily on the profit to be obtained from the supply of agricultural products. The profit depends on the intensity with which the land can be worked before the marginal cost exceeds the value of the product. If prices rise relatively to costs, then more can be produced, total profits will be higher and the price of land will rise. If the prices of agricultural products fall or other costs rise, there will be a smaller profit, the price of land will fall and the least fertile land may cease to be used. Since the supply of land exists independently of its value, its 'supply curve' can only be visualised as a vertical line on which the average price is determined by the profit derived from the total production. It is of course likely that the effective area of land can be increased, if need be, by embankment, drainage, irrigation or reclamation, so that the supply of land is not entirely irresponsive to its price; but the area added in this way is likely to be such a minute fraction of the existing land that it has little effect on the general principle.

The profit on which the price of land depends is the difference between total receipts and the total costs incurred, at the most profitable level of cultivation and including in costs the basic expenses of the cultivating families. If the occupiers are tenants, the division of the profit between them and the owners will be determined mainly by the competition between tenants and would-be tenants for the limited number of farms. If there is a dense and increasing population with little alternative employment outside agriculture, then the force of competition may transfer almost all the surplus to the owners. And frequently in past history, such a conjunction has produced the social unrest which led in many countries to the elimination of land owners in favour of the far more numerous occupiers. But an increasing population, even of owner-occupiers, with no alternative employment in industry or commerce, will find the value of land rising as more people try to buy vacant farms or farms are sub-divided into smaller units thus giving a smaller output to each of a larger number of farming families. In some parts of Eastern Europe, the process has been taken a stage further and the owner-occupiers have themselves been forcibly converted into hired workers on farms owned and managed by State authority; but the same forces reappear when collective farms on good land make higher incomes for their workers than farms on poor land and a compulsory contribution is levied on each collective unit by the State.

In Ireland the classical theory of rent was precisely demonstrated by the relations between a dense peasant population increasing in numbers and a comparatively few landowners mostly of a different race or religion from their tenants. In a modified form, this pressure on land and the consequent rise in rents operated in Britain also up to the last quarter of the nineteenth century. It was this setting which produced the first legislation on land tenure designed to strengthen the bargaining power of the tenants and would-be tenants, the Agricultural Holdings Acts of 1875, 1883 and 1908; the process was continued until, under the Agricultural Holdings Act 1948, agricultural tenants had virtually a tenancy for life, subject only to attaining a minimum standard of efficient husbandry. But this rising tide of State regulation in Britain coincided first with a falling and then with a low tide of agricultural prosperity, temporarily interrupted only from 1914 to 1920. Land ceased to be scarce in Britain in relation to the demand for it, firstly because its products could be brought by sea from the newly settled continents; secondly, because a greater yield was obtained from the existing land at lower costs; and thirdly, because the agricultural population found a higher income in urban trades or in agriculture overseas. Consequently, rents were lower for agricultural land in 1940 than in 1870 (in spite of the higher costs for maintenance and improvements) because the profits to be obtained from it never again attained, except in war time, the levels reached in the mid-years of the nineteenth century.[1] As a further consequence, the ownership of agricultural land became one of the least profitable investments for capital, apart from the social and sporting amenities; from 1920 onwards, an increasing number of farms were sold by owners to their tenants until by 1939 some 30 per cent of the farms in this country were held by owner-occupiers. Twenty years later the proportion might well be over half.

Over these seventy years, therefore, both legislation and economic forces operated to depress the profits from, and the price of, agricultural land, whether expressed as rent or as land values. But after 1940 the marked rise in agricultural profits

[1] Central Landowners' Association. *Rent of Agricultural Land in England and Wales, 1870-1914* (1949).

associated with the war and post-war policy reversed this trend. The value of agricultural land sold with vacant possession rose steadily, an 'unearned increment' accruing to those who owned this scarce factor at the start of the trend; the value of land sold without vacant possession, subject to a tenancy agreement, rose much more slowly, since current legislation made it difficult to raise rents to match either the increasing costs of repairs or the increasing profits derived from the occupation of land (Table 15).

Table 15. *Median Price of Land per acre in England and Wales, 1937–55 (farms of 300–500 acres)*

	Farms sold			
	With vacant possession		With sitting tenant	
	Price	Index	Price	Index
	£		£	
1937–39	31·3	100	23·6	100
1949–51	94·9	305	45·6	197
1955	90·2	290	49·0	212

Source: J. T. Ward, 'Changes in the Sale Value of Farm Real Estate in England and Wales, 1937–9 to 1951', *Farm Economist*, vol. VII, No. 4 (1953), pp. 145–54; vol. VIII, No. 6 (1956), p. 52.

This differential in land values has developed because a policy of agricultural expansion has been combined with legislation hindering a rise in rents; it has thus intensified the trend towards owner-occupation, since the owner of a farm only obtains a greatly reduced value if he, or his executors, should have to sell during the currency of a tenancy. Hence, land-owners have a strong financial inducement either to sell when a farm falls vacant or to take it in hand and farm themselves. It is a curious result of legislation designed to increase the bargaining power of tenants that it has stimulated the decline in the number of farms to be let and therefore in the number of tenant farmers.

It is, however, remarkable that so great an expansion in agricultural output has been achieved with a comparatively small rise in land values, even on land sold with vacant possession.[1] Between 1937–9 and the mid 1950's, the net output

[1] The value of agricultural land in an industrial country is also influenced by many non-agricultural factors which are not discussed here.

of British agriculture rose by about one-half; farming profits increased six-fold, from about £60 millions to £310 millions; but the value of agricultural land with vacant possession barely trebled, showing a smaller rise than wholesale prices in general over this period. The actual area of land under crops and grass fell, but improved techniques, a higher standard of management all round, more fertilisers and more machinery enabled farmers to increase output per acre to an extent that would have appeared impossible a generation ago. And because land-ownership has become more widely diffused than in the past, a rise in land values arouses less opposition from parties of the left and, indeed, appears to be no longer a political problem; the far greater growth in other forms of capital—industrial, financial and commercial—has markedly reduced the relative importance of land-ownership as a base for exceptional chances of wealth or political power.

But there is one aspect of land unaffected by such agricultural improvements. Because land is primarily space, there may be acute scarcity of land in a particular locality where propinquity is valuable—near the Bank of England; at the junction of High Street and Main Street in any town; along a railway, a canal or a trunk road. Hence the owners of these sites may be able to extract very high prices for the use of their property, since there is a large difference between the profits expected from building on the favoured land and from buildings situated some distance away. Every expansion in the business done in a town's centre increases the value of the sites there and increases also the value of the sites on its edge as they become 'ripe for development' from agricultural to urban use. Since this rise in land values occurs as a result of the growth of the community as a whole, it is logical to argue that it should accrue to the community as a whole and not to the few who happen to own the favoured sites at the appropriate time. That argument was strongly supported by Henry George (1838–97) from his observation on the course of land values in the United States; he proposed a tax payable on every revaluation of land equal to amount of the increase from a given date. By the Town and Country Planning Act, 1947, a rather similar measure was introduced into the United Kingdom; a tax at 100 per cent was payable on any rise in values on a change in the use of land, whether or not there had been a change in ownership. The repeal of this legislation six years later was no doubt partly the result of a change in Government between the two dates but nevertheless it is instructive to observe the great difficulties which this legislation encountered in its brief life. In the first place, persons wishing to change the use of their own property found themselves liable to a special tax which might deter them from a change beneficial both to themselves and to society in general. Secondly, there remained no inducement to the owner of a given piece of land to sell at all, or to sell to the buyer offering the highest price who might be presumed to be putting the land to the most profitable use. Consequently there was little land offered for sale; public authorities had to use their powers of compulsory purchase, and private buyers found themselves paying more than the existing use value to the seller as well as the development charge to the State. And thirdly, the existing use value from which the charge was calculated was itself indeterminate; its value to the actual owner might include a wide range of personal preferences and prospects which influenced the price he might have paid for it or the price for which he would be prepared to sell, but such non-monetary factors were necessarily ignored by any official valuer. The tax was therefore arbitrary in its incidence and its collection seriously impeded the working of a highly important market, just as the legislation on land tenure has impeded the market in tenanted farms, to the detriment of the would-be tenants.

II. THE SUPPLY OF LAND TO EACH FARMER

The owner of a factory wishing to expand his business can either buy another as it stands, or add an extension to his existing building, or begin afresh on a new site with a new building. A farmer wishing to expand his farm can only do so, in a settled country, by taking over some other farmer's business, either in whole or part; unless large technical improvements are possible, farmers can only feed more cows by feeding fewer sheep, and grow more wheat by growing less grass. Hence most farmers have to take the existing shape and area of their farm as a fixed factor; only if their capital and managerial ability are quite out of scale with their existing holding will they alter the size of their business by moving to some other farm. But once a major decision of this sort is taken, their production planning starts with the given area of land, its roads, water and buildings, the rent that has to be paid for it or the interest on the mortgage required to buy it.

For most farmers, therefore, the area of land under their control is fixed; and most farmers would pay the current market price, either in rent or value, for any extra land in the vicinity of their farms, if it was obtainable. This in itself shows that the men on the smaller farms, on any one of the 185,000 farms in Great Britain between 5 and 50 acres in size, are up against diminishing returns in a real way. From a sample of East Anglian farms (excluding fen farms) it has been possible to calculate the net output per acre required in the circumstances of the nineteen-fifties to obtain an income of £500 a year, after allowing for the costs incurred in producing that

Table 16. *Net output required to produce £500 in farm income*

Farm size (acres)	Total (£)	Per acre (£)
20	1,164	58·2
30	1,329	44·3
40	1,494	37·4
50	1,659	33·2
60	1,824	30·4
70	1,989	28·4
80	2,154	26·9
90	2,319	25·8
100	2,484	24·8

Net output = sales (adjusted for valuation changes) less purchase of livestock, seeds and feeds.

Source: F. G. Sturrock and D. B. Wallace, *The Family Farm*, Department of Agriculture, Farm Economics Branch, Occasional Papers No. 4, p. 13 (Cambridge, 1956).

output (Table 16). The production from 20–30 acres of an output which will provide a net income over costs of £400–£500 involves the application of labour, fertilisers and capital to a degree which may defeat its own object through increasing costs. It is this invariable input of one important factor—

land—which gives European agriculture its peculiar economic structure, of a large number of small family businesses each set in a rigid framework. Hence arises the general pre-occupation with output per acre, for as the standard of living rises outside farming, as farmers come to desire the industrial goods which can only be bought by increasing cash incomes, the pressure to expand output also increases; technical improvements are adopted to offset the effect of diminishing returns which result from applying variable inputs of other factors to a fixed area of land.

In a completely static society, one might assume that over a long period the sizes of holdings would become adjusted to provide (with current techniques) a range of farm incomes adapted to the range of incomes in other occupations. But few societies have been completely static. A society whose area of land and whose cultivating techniques are both static is likely to have also a rising population which requires the continuing sub-division of holdings into smaller and more numerous units, until many are too small to provide even a bare subsistence. Such was the situation in Ireland up to 1850 and such is the situation in such countries as Yugoslavia and Egypt today. A developing society, whose average income per head outside farming is rising, is likely to find itself with numbers of problem farms, too small even with improved techniques to provide what is currently regarded as a reasonable income. Of course, if farmers and farm families moved freely into other occupations where their chances of higher incomes were greater, such problem farms would be gradually eliminated by amalgamation into larger units; it is ultimately the stickiness of the human element in farming which maintains a large and continuing disparity of incomes between agriculture and other occupations, by maintaining in farming families with inadequate land. It is interesting to note the very different situation in the United States, where over the last half-century the area under cultivation has risen and the number of farms has fallen, so that the area of land per farm has markedly increased (Table 17). The average size of farm was 140–150 acres in 1920 and 240–250 acres in 1954, an expansion obtained both by adding nearly three million acres to the area of farm land and by the

Table 17. *Number of farms and land in farms in the United States,*
1910–54

	No. of farms (thousands)	Land in farms (million acres)
1910	6,362	878·8
1920	6,448	955·9
1930	6,289	986·8
1940	6,097	1,060·9
1950	5,382	1,158·6
1954	4,782	1,158·2

Source: U.S. Census of Agriculture, 1954.

amalgamation of existing holdings. This last process has been most rapid since 1940, when industrial prosperity has drawn into other occupations more than a million farm families. In such a setting, the input of land is perhaps more flexible than the input of labour, whose scarcity is the dominant factor in farm planning and certainly in farm mechanisation.

The extent to which individual farmers can alter their input of land, the degree of flexibility in farm boundaries, the terms on which land can be obtained, these are likely to be dominated not by details of land tenure, but by the general characteristics of the society as a whole and the stage it has reached in its economic development. Almost any form of land tenure can work in a favourable environment, where income per head is rising and there is rough equality of bargaining power between the parties concerned. No form of land tenure, however perfect in theory, can prevent extreme poverty among occupiers whose numbers are increasing faster than the area of land or the volume of alternative employments. Nevertheless, types of land tenure are important since they can both aggrevate a bad situation and hinder the development of desirable technical changes.

III. TYPES OF LAND TENURE

We may classify the main types of land tenure as follows:

1. Owner-occupation
   (a) unrestricted
   (b) land use restricted by State
   (c) land use restricted by common rights
   (d) restricted entry

2. Individual tenancy
   (a) classified by lease
      (i) for life
      (ii) on contract
      (iii) at will
      (iv) through intermediaries
   (b) classified by functions
      (i) tenant providing labour
      (ii) tenant providing labour and working capital
      (iii) tenant providing labour and all equipment
3. Communal tenure
   (a) shifting arable cultivation
   (b) grazing rights
   (c) restricted public use—parks, nature reserves etc.
4. Communal ownership
   (a) communal farming
   (b) individual tenancy

When the forms of tenure are thus set out, it becomes clear that few countries follow one type only, and many of these types can be found side by side today in a country such as Britain. Many hill farms and most crofts have common grazing rights; many farmers hold individual tenancies from public bodies such as County Councils or the Duchy of Cornwall or the Agricultural Land Commission; tenancy in many forms combines with the ultimate aim of owner-occupation in the United States and New Zealand; in Britain, probably half the farms are owned by their occupiers and half held on contract by tenants whose rights and duties are defined by legislation. The dominant types of land tenure in each country are the results partly of history and partly of geographical factors peculiar to each country. One would not expect, for instance, to find similar customs in a country long settled for arable farming and in a pastoral economy of nomadic tribes with their grazing animals; in a country with a long history of law and commercial contracts and in a society of primitive tribes scattered over largely uncultivated land. Hence it is not easy to discuss land tenure in general terms, since its problems are so closely related both to a particular stage of economic development and to the peculiar conditions of land use. But by drawing on the experience of British history, with side glances at land tenure in some of the countries settled by

British emigrants, we can get some understanding of the relationship between land tenure, social development and agricultural policy.

1. THE OCCUPYING OWNER

The historical evolution of European agriculture produced the political ideal of owner-occupation, with the cultivator freed from all dues, whether in cash, kind or service, to a separate owner. The 'magic of property which turns sand into gold' was a potent force in the successive revolutions from 1779 onwards which led in most countries to the extinction of land-owning as a separate function; owner-occupation became therefore the basis for the newly settled countries in America and Australasia. The ownership of land by the farmer in clear and undisputable title was found to give, in most circumstances, the maximum of security for the farm family, and the maximum of benefit to the community by way of increased output through the investment of capital and the adoption of technical improvements. But there are a number of qualifications to this general rule.

If an increasing population is farming a fixed area of land with primitive techniques and few alternative employments, the benefits of ownership may be merely temporary or even derisory; the inevitable sub-division of holdings to accommodate the increasing number of farm families only ensures an equal share in poverty; it will also hinder the adoption of improved cultivations or a proper rotation of restorative with exhaustive crops. Rapid industrialisation seems the only remedy for such an agricultural situation which was common over much of Europe into the twentieth century. Only when the surplus of partially employed farm families has been absorbed into urban employments can some form of land reform be applied to combine the smaller holdings into more economic units. The process may occur as a result of market forces, or it may involve some control over the inflow of potential farmers or over sales of existing holdings.

Especially where primitive cultivators are being introduced to a modern economy, unrestricted ownership of land by individuals can lead to the adoption of destructive systems of farming; or to the expropiation of a backward tribe before their more advanced neighbours. Technical ignorance, or the existence of peoples at widely differing levels of culture may both be valid reasons for restricting owners from various actions deemed undesirable, whether in matters of cultivation or in aggregation of land. At the same time such protective action in the interests either of the community as a whole or of one particularly weak section of it runs the risk of hampering the energetic and innovating individual; nor will such action be effective unless the administration is reasonably efficient and honest.

The right to own land has usually carried with it the right to farm as badly as the owner likes, even to the extent of leaving land uncultivated, eroded or weed-infested; in the newly settled countries, early settlers frequently took up more land than they could farm or graze in the hopes partly of extending their operations later and partly of selling on a rising market to future immigrants. But as land becomes scarce in relation to the demand for it, public opinion becomes more concerned over its misuse or lack of use by existing owners; unrestricted rights of ownership may be found to clash with political ideals of a farm for every family; or the rights of neighbours not to be over-run with rabbits or brambles; or the right of the community to have a scarce resource put to its most economic use. For although market forces may eventually remove through bankruptcy the less efficient farmer and the squatter who leaves his land uncultivated, the process may take more time than public opinion will tolerate and may involve permanent damage to the land and therefore increase the future costs of agricultural output. It is therefore logical, if not always politically feasible, to require of owner-occupiers certain minimum standards of efficiency in their use of land, with the threat of dispossession in the event of failure to attain those standards. In Britain, legislation to this effect was in force during the second world war and was continued under the Agriculture Act, 1947 until 1958; the administration was carried out by the local officers of the Ministry of Agriculture, in conjunction with the Agricultural Executive Committees. In other countries, control has not gone so far and usually includes only prohibitions against the harbouring of dangerous weeds and pests, or changes in land use which may affect much wider areas than one farm, such as works of irrigation or drainage or urban development.

There may be many valid reasons why owners of land may be unwilling or unable to cultivate it themselves, so that tenancy in some form or another is common even in countries based on owner-occupation. And tenancy has obvious advantages for the young man on his way up the ladder of modern farming, since it greatly reduces the amount of capital required to enter the profession. In the United States, for instance, between one quarter and two-fifths of farms have been held by a variety of tenancy in the current century, the proportion rising in times of agricultural depression and falling in times of prosperity.[1]

2. INDIVIDUAL TENANCY

If there is reasonable equality of bargaining power between land owners and their tenants or prospective tenants, the terms made between them for the use of land are likely to represent a reasonable compromise between the owners' wishes for a high income, maintenance of land fertility and freedom to obtain repossession of the land if required, and the tenants' wishes for a high income, freedom to cultivate as is found best, and security for the business to continue. But any tenancy involves some measure of dual responsibility over which disputes can easily arise; written contracts with access to an efficient system of commercial justice can be regarded as the minimum requirement for the proper working of a tenancy system in the complex conditions of modern farming.

The terms of the bargain between owner and occupier can vary greatly, partly because of the nature of the farming, partly because of local custom and tradition. The English copyholder usually had a lease for life, or for three lives, of a bare holding; buildings, fences and drains were often the responsibility of the tenant, who paid a stated sum every year plus a further sum at the succession of each life. That type of contract was replaced in the nineteenth century by the custom of a lease, either for a

[1] United States Census of Agriculture, 1954.

certain term of years or for an indefinite period subject to notice on either side; the owner usually provided the permanent buildings and kept them in repair, and often bound his tenant to follow certain prescribed crop rotations in order to preserve the fertility of the farm. In the United States and New Zealand, the owner may also provide some of the working capital in the form of machinery, fertilisers, seeds or the herd of dairy cows; the rent is then expressed as a fixed sum plus some stated share of the gross or net receipts. There is no reason to expect that any one type of contract will be universally or continuously the best.

If there is not reasonable equality of bargaining power between owners and tenants, the pressure of competition for a limited area of land can produce gross inequality of terms; there may be high rents, extreme poverty among occupiers with no security of tenure, little compensation for any improvements made by them, and little inducement for such improvements to be made either by tenants or owners. In such circumstances, legislation properly administered by a strong central government can somewhat rectify the lack of bargaining power by the tenants; compensation for tenants' improvements and reasonable notice to quit can be enforced, and in certain circumstances it is possible to control rents by arbitration or by some administrative body, such as the Scottish Land Court, which controls rents on crofts and small holdings. But if the price paid for land is not to be fixed in the open market, a number of problems develop. Tenants for vacant holdings have to be selected by some other criterion than ability to pay the highest rent; a reasonable level of rents has to be established on an arbitrary basis; land owners may not be willing to continue to function under the new conditions and further measures may be required to expedite a transition to owner-occupation. Then the competition for land may take the form of high values for vacant farms which in turn may cause heavy indebtedness among owner-occupiers; new distinctions in income are created between those tenants protected by administrative measures and those who have bought on borrowed money because they were rejected as tenants. The control of rents when efficiently administered has in the past brought a considerable transference of income from owners to tenants, but it clearly increases rather than diminishes the competition for land. For the pressure of population which lies behind this competition cannot be abolished by administrative measures but only by the gradual investment of capital in industry and public services which in turn creates new wealth and alternative sources of employment.

3. COMMUNAL OWNERSHIP

A large area of farm land in the United Kingdom, over a million acres, is publicly owned by various bodies, the Crown Estate, the Duchy of Cornwall, the Duchy of Lancaster, the Forestry Commission, the Agricultural Land Commission, and County Councils; other land is held as an investment by financial trusts, the Ecclesiastical Commissioners, universities, colleges, schools and charitable organisations. Given a reasonable and well-defined system of land tenure, farming by individuals can function successfully under such ownership, which can provide greater continuity and sometimes more expert management than private owners. There is nothing inherently impossible in a system of communal or State ownership of land, organised through professional land agents, combined with farming by selected tenants; indeed, such a system might function more efficiently than private ownership where farming depends on complicated systems of irrigation or drainage. But these physical problems have not been important in western Europe except in small areas, and the occupying owner has become the norm; the advantages of undivided responsibility and the political independence of Government which ownership gives have outweighed in most countries the advantages of large-scale land management which clearly requires a highly developed system of control.

4. COMMUNAL FARMING

Communal farming has not been of importance in western Europe with its tradition of family farms combining livestock and crops in small units. But company farms are well established in the United Kingdom; they have also undertaken much pioneer work in tropical countries in developing the output of tea, coffee, cocoa, rubber, sugar and sisal; the structure of a limited liability company enabled such estates to draw their capital through the London Stock Exchange and thus to finance larger units than could be achieved by individuals. Between the wars, the Land Settlement Association also experimented in Britain with grouped small-holdings on which tenants, selected from men long unemployed, ran individual enterprises with the advantages of centralised supervision, marketing and some production services. Both these forms are, however, exceptional to the usual patterns of British farming, the occupying owner and the tenant holding from a personal or corporate landlord, within the framework of custom and agricultural law.

IV. THE SUPPLY OF CAPITAL

Capital can be broadly defined as goods employed but not used up in the course of production, together with the money or credit which gives power to buy such goods. A farmer's capital may consist therefore of

1. fixed capital, the land and the buildings on it, if he is a free-holder;
2. his working capital, tractors, machinery, breeding stock, etc;
3. his financial capital, his balance or overdraft at the bank, his shares in some company, his life assurance.

The distinction between the first two types of capital is partly one of time, it will be observed; both a building and a tractor eventually fall to bits, but while one may outlast several generations of men, the working life of a tractor is normally not much more than a decade. But the distinction also rests partly on the degree of physical separation; farm buildings, roads, and drains are integral parts of the farm on which they were constructed, while combines and cows are moveable.

The annual addition to the nation's capital depends partly on the size of the annual output of goods and services, and partly on the willingness of its nationals to forego present consumption for the sake of an increase in the future output. In 1958 the flow of goods and services in the United Kingdom was valued at £20,000 millions; of these, about £3,600 millions, or about 18 per cent, were devoted to the upkeep of the existing capital and to additions to the stock, the two not being

Table 18. *Investment in the United Kingdom, 1958*

£ million

1. Housing   581
2. Manufacturing   895
3. Gas, electricity, water   384
4. Transport and communications   467
5. Distribution, road transport, etc.   549
6. Social services   184
7. Agriculture, forestry, fishing   127

Source: *National Income and Expenditure, 1959*, p. 53.

distinguished in the national accounts. Table 18 shows how the greater part of these resources were used. These investments imply that people, companies and various forms of Government did not spend all their incomes on current consumption; and that people, companies and various forms of Government decided to use these resources thus saved in the proportions indicated above.

It is a basic part of the theory of a free market economy that the allocation of new investment should, as a rule, depend on the relative level of expected profits; the various Stock Exchanges and the banking system provide the central market through which the individual savings are canalised for distribution according to this criterion. If one particular branch of industry is making a large surplus over costs, then it is probable (though not certain) that resources invested there will add a higher value of the future output of goods and services than resources invested in an industry whose goods are less urgently demanded. This general rule has two important qualifications. There are important, though non-monetary, advantages to be derived from investment in hospitals, schools, nature reserves, playing grounds and other forms of social capital, so that some investment must proceed on a rough and highly subjective estimate of relative urgency of needs which cannot be expressed in terms of money. Secondly, where companies invest their own savings in the expansion of their own business, the weighing up of expected profits may occur only over a narrow field.

The share of this national flow of resources which is annually invested in farming is determined partly by thousands of farmers each making his own decision on the expected profits in the foreseeable future; partly by the amount of financial capital they can command, including what they can borrow from other people who are willing to lend to them. Let us take each of these factors in turn.

If a farmer has £1,000 to spare, he can spend it on a cruise or on his house, he can invest it in Government stocks and thus increase his future income, or he can buy a pedigree bull or a grass dryer in the hopes of raising the value of his output in years to come and increasing his income in that way. His choice between immediate and future consumption is likely to be determined as much by personal preferences as economic factors; but his choice between Government stocks, a pedigree bull and a grass dryer is likely to be influenced mainly by economic considerations, by the expected returns from each of these investments over its future life, and the degree of risk attached both to the probable income and to the capital. The expected returns from any specific item of fixed capital depend on estimates of future trends in demand, of other sources of supply and of probable technical developments in production; some allowance must be made if low chances of a very high income have to be weighed against higher chances of a more moderate but stable return; there may also be different waiting times before expected increases in income can occur. Pig production can be expanded within a year, if the market is favourable, and the scale of production can be altered without substantially altering the rest of the farm business; but to plant an orchard involves a delay of 3–5 years before the increment of output can be obtained, during which costs will be incurred and markets may change, and the field is debarred from crop production while the trees remain. Many investment decisions must clearly be made on a very superficial judgment of probabilities, heavily weighted by personal preferences; nevertheless, farmers, like other business men, do tend to invest their resources in enterprises which are the most profitable in the current period, or which they have reason to believe will shortly become more profitable than others. The steady expansion in dairy herds and the milk output over the last 25 years is an obvious case in point, as is the rapid rise in pig herds from 1949 onwards. And on a rational calculation, such investment should be made along each of the various farm enterprises until the expected net return from £100 invested in each is approximately equal.

But once capital has been invested, then a different set of considerations comes into play in deciding whether or not to continue production at the new level. If the orchard has been established, then whether the original expectation of increased income materialises or no, it will be kept in production so long as the returns exceed the specific costs of spraying, pruning and picking and there is no alternative use for the land which would yield greater profits, allowing for the costs of grubbing out the trees. Hence net profits of apple growing can fall to comparatively low levels for a long period of time before there is much diminution in supply which may indeed only fall because trees eventually die and there has been no new planting. Orchards, field drains and many buildings are extreme instances of this type of fixed capital; once the investment has been made, it loses its identity and becomes merged into the farm, as an integral part of the larger asset. But even where the investment retains its identity, once it has been made its value depends, not on its original cost, but on the revenue it is likely to earn in the foreseeable future, which may be very different from the revenue expected when the investment was made. Expected returns in the near future thus determine both the pattern of current investment and the market value of past investment.

The supply of financial capital available for current investment is thus influenced partly by the size of the national income, partly by the proportion which the community, as individuals or collectively, decide not to spend on current consumption. The size of current investment in agriculture is influenced, therefore, partly by the total level of current investment, partly by the relative profitability of farming and other competing trades, partly by the extent to which the supply of capital flows easily between its various sources and its various uses.

Individual farmers can draw on:

1. the capital they own;
2. the savings from annual income;
3. non-commercial loans from family or friends;
4. commercial loans.

The man on a small farm, the young farmer starting on his way up, the agricultural worker hoping for his own farm, are not likely to have much capital of their own nor to be earning an income large enough to save much from it. They may be able to borrow, but their own lack of capital and their low incomes limit the security they can offer; for the potential lender must consider the extreme variability of agricultural incomes, resulting partly from chances of weather and disease, and partly from the variability of management among small units; he is likely to offset the risks to his capital and to the regularity of the income from his loan by asking for a high rate of interest and some independent security. The established and successful farmers with accumulated capital and high incomes can usually borrow on the security both of their personal reputation and their existing capital, whether in land or stock. In this country, short-term credit, to cover the seasonal gap between planting and harvesting or to buy fertilisers or livestock, can usually be obtained on commercial terms from the commercial banks, or from the merchants who buy farmers' produce or supply their requisites. Long-term loans to buy farms or to finance durable improvements can sometimes be obtained locally in the form of mortgages, or from specialised institutions such as the Agricultural Mortgage Corporation or the Scottish Agricultural Securities Corporation Ltd; such loans are usually only available to owners of farms who can offer the freehold of their property as security. Hence the supply both of short-term loans and of long-term capital to any individual farmer may be strictly limited or available only at high cost. And if borrowing becomes inevitable—if a farmer must borrow to buy his land, to finance the harvesting of his main crop, to buy his basic livestock, or to tide over a crop failure—then the high interest rate may cripple his enterprise; he may have too little income left to pay off the capital of his debt, to finance improvements, or to survive another bad season. Any period of widespread misfortune in agriculture is likely to leave behind it a number of farmers heavily burdened with debt incurred in this way, and desperately short both of capital and of credit.

In primitive conditions, debt is general among cultivators, and the local money-lender, who is often the local merchant as well, becomes the real controller of the local economy through his control of this essential but scarce commodity. In such circumstances, the shortage in agriculture of capital and of seasonal credit is only a reflection of the general scarcity in the economy as a whole, which results from general poverty. And it is that general scarcity which also produces the high rates of interest common in undeveloped countries. But in all economies, the ability of farmers to borrow, even for profitable uses, is more limited than the ability of industry, partly because of the small size of the borrowing unit, partly because of the extreme variability of income and of management. These disabilities can be diminished by a variety of institutions. In some countries, co-operative credit banks have been able to secure loans from outside agriculture on the joint security of a group of farmers who personally supervise the use made by their members of such credits. In the United Kingdom during the last war, the Agricultural Executive Committees supplied goods and services on credit to needy farmers whose operations were closely supervised. Such a combination of lending and supervision obviously reduces the risks of rash borrowing and of mis-use of loans, though the cost of supervision may itself be quite appreciable. Again, there are large works of irrigation, drainage, afforestation or reconstruction involving many farms which might well yield an economic return in total, but which are not likely to be carried out without a high degree of co-operation, either voluntary or compelled.

In framing agricultural policy, therefore, it is important to realise that many farmers may be unable, for any of a variety of reasons, to find the capital or credit to invest in improvements or in adaptations, which in themselves might quite likely yield an economic return. And, on the other hand, recent studies have shown that some farmers who could borrow for obvious improvements are held back by over-caution, or by an inherited dislike of running into debt for any reason at all; tenant farmers are further handicapped if their land owners are unable or unwilling to make periodic investments and they themselves have no security to offer as the basis of long-term loans. Such peculiarities of the farming structure may well hinder agriculture in competing for the limited amount of commercial capital and credit available for all uses; and if co-operative societies, or State-sponsored credit banks, or well-administered State grants can render the market less imperfect, there will be a general benefit.

Further Reading

F.A.O. Agricultural Studies:
> No. 17, *Communal Land Tenure* (1953).
> No. 35, *Improving Agricultural Tenancy* (1957).
> No. 39, *The Owner-Cultivator in a Progressive Agriculture* (1958).

State of Food and Agriculture, 1957 (Rome, 1957), Section IV.

'Capital and Credit in Agriculture', *International Journal of Agrarian Affairs,* vol. II, Nos. 3, 4 (1957).

'Redistribution of Farm Land in Seven Countries', *International Journal of Agrarian Affairs,* vol. II, No. 1 (1955).

D. Warriner, *Land Reform and Development in the Middle East* (R.I.I.A., 1957).

S. Hooper, *The Finance of Farming in Great Britain* (Europa Publications Ltd., 1955).

J. T. Ward, *Farm Rents and Tenure* (Estates Gazette Ltd., 1959).

D. R. Denman and V. F. Stewart, *Farm Rents* (Allen and Unwin, 1959).

CHAPTER VII

THE SUPPLY OF LABOUR AND OF MANAGERS

I. THE SUPPLY OF LABOUR

The supply of land is mainly a physical feature, though the value of that land is partly influenced by the actions of men in providing communications or drainage or water or fertilisers. The supply of capital, expressed in terms of money or of bricks and mortar, depends on the actions of human beings over the past and in the present. But when we consider the supply of labour, we are considering the humans themselves—the motives which lead them to choose one job rather than another, to choose this place rather than that in which to make a home for themselves and their families.

Expected income is the first influence to be considered on the number of persons employed in different occupations. Other things being equal, one would expect that people would tend to move out of occupations where incomes were below average and into occupations where incomes were above average, thus tending to reduce such differentials. But this simple statement, though broadly true, is subject to wide qualifications. In the first place, more people tend to become barristers or gold diggers or uranium prospectors than is warranted by the average income earned in these occupations. The chance of a very high income exercises more attraction than is warranted by the much more frequent low income. Secondly, many occupations carry with them subsidiary benefits—board and lodging, a free house, pensions, expense allowances and the like. Particularly in a period of high taxation these benefits may exercise a marked influence on recruitment. Others carry disadvantages, living in with the employer, or occupying a bad house with no security of tenure. Thirdly, in choosing a job, people also choose the environment in which, and the companions with which, they will spend a large part of their lives. A friendly team, routine work, absence of responsibility and regular pay may, for one man, be adequate compensation for a relatively low income; 'being one's own boss' and the social status of a farmer keeps many small-holders working for long hours for a smaller cash income than many hired workers on large farms. Such rewards are not less real because they cannot easily be measured against money by anyone except the individuals concerned. We cannot ignore them, nor the importance of personal characteristics which cause one man to become a research scientist and another a farmer, largely irrespective of the financial motives. But the relative income to be expected from different occupations is clearly the most important factor in influencing the flow of people between occupations; and we may for the moment consider that in isolation from the others.

If all human beings were identical and there were no barriers to mobility, both geographical and occupational, we could expect the working population to be employed in such a way that earnings were roughly equal. If the demand for one product rose, so that incomes earned in that trade rose, more people would move into it, either as hired men in response to higher wages or as independent workers in response to higher profits; earnings in that trade would tend to fall again as output increased and the number of workers rose; earnings elsewhere would tend to rise, to check the outflow of people, and an approximate equality of earnings would again be established. We could expect constant shifts in the numbers employed between occupations, as demand for the final products changed, as technical inventions altered the proportions in which the factors of production were combined for any given output.

In this unreal world of identical and mobile robots, we can imagine that the level of wages in each industry or craft might be negotiated somewhat after the present fashion through trade unions bargaining with the managers, either firm by firm, or for each industry. The upper limit to each bargain would be set by 'what the trade would stand'—composed partly of the elasticity of demand for the end product in the face of a rise in price after a rise in costs; partly of the possible substitution of other and now cheaper tools in the place of trade union members; and thirdly, on the power of each trade union to protect its own members from competition by other robots, flocking to the factory gate to offer their services at something less than the new rate of pay.

But human beings are not identical and their movement over space and between occupations is restricted by a huge variety of impediments—restricted abilities, difficult temperaments, the cost of travel, fear of unemployment, lack of housing, unwillingness to break ties of family or friendship, differences in education, speech, race, religion or caste. These barriers divide even the nationals of one state into groups which may be virtually non-competing; the market for labour is fragmented; each town or region, each occupation or craft may have its own price level, reflecting the conditions of supply and demand peculiar to itself. The poorer and more primitive a society, the stronger usually are such barriers between groups and the weaker the competition between them, even though there may be strong competition within each group for the limited jobs offered. Hence there may be substantial differences in earnings between regions for the same type of work; and substantial differences also within the same area between occupations, entry into which is perhaps restricted to members of a particular race, or certain families. The difficulty of breaking into such restricted but higher paid occupations then intensifies the pressure of supply in those directions where entry is not controlled and wages are low, thus intensifying the disparity in earnings.

The relative level of earnings of hired workers in British farming has been peculiarly depressed over the last century by a combination of such adverse factors. In the hundred years from 1841, the population of Great Britain increased from about 18½ millions to nearly 47 millions. During this time, there were always more boys looking for jobs than there were old men dying or retiring, and this rising tide of job seekers would, in country districts, flow naturally into agriculture. But even in the middle years of last century, the expansion in agricultural employment was slow; while from 1875 onwards (with the exception of the years of war) employment was declining, under the influence of rising imports and falling prices for agricultural products, and of more and better machinery. Over most of the nineteenth century, farmers could find, at a rate of pay less than that common in towns, all the men they wished to employ; the average rate of pay in each district was set roughly by the distance from large centres of urban employment (Tables 19, 20). Low wages, casual earnings and intermittent destitution were common both for farm workers and for the

Table 19. *Average weekly cash wages of farm workers in England, 1768–1910*

	1768/70	1837	1869/70	1898	1910
	s. d.	s. d.	s. d.	s. d.	s. d.
Eastern counties	7 6	10 4	11 3	12 8	14 0
South-east and east midland counties ..	7 11	10 0	12 5	13 10	15 1
West midland and south-west counties ..	6 10	8 10	10 10	12 11	13 9
Northern counties ..	6 4	12 1	15 0	16 11	18 0

Source: Lord Ernle, *English Farming* (Longmans, 1912), Appendix X.

unskilled workers of the towns; the resulting poverty led to marked stratification within the wage-earning class, since education or apprenticeships were only possible for a minority of the better paid craftsmen. And within agriculture, the comparative isolation of each group of farms and the nature of the individual bargaining between each farmer and his few men brought a wide dispersal of earnings about the averages for each region or county. In such circumstances, trade unions could do little for the farm workers except to spread information on current rates of wages, to assist mobility, and to take up the occasional case of gross underpayment. Later, from 1924 onwards, their representatives played an important part on the Agricultural Wages Board and the county Wages Committees which undertook the negotiation of minimum wages between farmers and the farm workers; the legal enforcement of such negotiated minimums had considerable effect between the wars in evening up the lowest paid wages which might result from the unequal bargaining power between the two parties to individual bargains.

During the two world wars, and in the years of inflation which followed the second, unemployment disappeared and the shortage of unskilled labour led to a marked rise in the lowest range of wages, both absolutely and in relation to wages of other grades. Wider opportunities of education, less marked divergences between regions and classes in customs and speech, better and cheaper transport have all helped to reduce the barriers to geographical and occupational mobility. These trends would naturally lead to a reduction in the differentials between wage classes, as the supply of labour moved more freely into those occupations which hitherto had commanded earnings above the average. The relative rise in the earnings of unskilled workers, compared with the years before 1914, was marked even in the period of unemployment between the wars, as an enduring result of the scarcity of such labour during the first world war; and the process was intensified from 1940 onwards. An even more marked reduction in inequalities might have occurred save for two important developments; the shortage of housing which greatly limited geographical mobility; and the determination of the unions of the better paid workers to preserve their differentials over the lower paid workers. It is noteworthy that in the post-war years, the major disputes have occurred over problems of differentials—whether or not a customary differential should be reduced or maintained or increased. As the largest of the lowest paid industries, agriculture has been especially involved in this struggle to raise the relative level of wages; some success was achieved during the second world war but since then, the rise in the agricultural minimum wage and in agricultural earnings has barely kept pace with the increase in earnings in industry (Fig. 6, p. 141). In a period of full employment and general inflation, when all wage rates were rising, farm workers managed to follow the general trend, though not to alter their relative position. But the continuation of the differential encouraged also the continued drift of farm workers out of

Table 20. *Number of agricultural workers in Great Britain, 1851, 1911, 1931, 1951, in thousands*

	1851	1911	1931	1951
Farmers	303	279	294	302
Farmers' relatives	136	142	95	108
Regular workers	1,473	794	628	544
Other workers	89	166	145	155
Total	2,001	1,381	1,162	1,109

Source: J. R. Bellerby, 'Distribution of Manpower in Agriculture and Industry, 1851–1951', *Farm Economist*, vol. IX, No. 1 (1958), pp. 1–11.

agriculture, and this drift in turn encouraged farmers to pay higher wages to those who remained and to raise their productivity by further mechanisation, by new buildings and by better management.

II. THE SUPPLY OF MANAGERS

Although the market for farm workers may be dispersed and imperfect, yet the forces of supply and demand do create, in a small and unified country such as Great Britain, something approaching a market price, of which the minimum wage agreed by the Wages Board provides a floor. But the market for farmers is a less conspicuous affair, in which economic influences operate in still more devious ways.

In a commercialised economy, the demand for farmers is derived from the prices paid for agricultural products, from the aggregate net farming income which results when all costs of production have been deducted from the gross receipts. The supply of farmers is derived, within a given population, from all those persons who ever thought that they might like to farm; but the number of persons actually farming is determined at any one time by the area of land available, the numbers and sizes of farms, the terms on which those farms can be acquired, and the prospects of obtaining a better livelihood in other trades.

The prospects of obtaining income as a farmer are presumably deduced from the actual incomes of those in that occupation. From the Ministry of Agriculture's publication

Farm Incomes 1957/8 it can be deduced that farms under 50 acres earned about £600 of net income, not much more than the earnings of a skilled farm worker; farms up to 100 acres obtained between £800 and £900, while farms of 500 acres and over obtained on an average about £4,250. On a different classification, about 5 per cent of the sample made a loss; between a fifth and a quarter made a modest income not exceeding £600; and about 7 per cent earned over £4,000. These incomes are the net profit of the farms, the sums which remunerated farmers for their manual work and management and which supplied interest on their capital, valued at rather more than £30 per acre. It is clear that the smaller farms are unlikely to provide incomes that could be earned by an average worker in other trades, though successful farmers on the larger farms were probably as well off as other people of comparable ability. Yet there is no lack of would-be tenants or buyers for these small farms, nor were there fewer farmers in the depressed years between the wars. Why do men seek to enter a trade whose earnings are variable and relatively low, even if it has a number of non-monetary advantages?

In a country such as Britain, there are apparently three main sources of farmers. The smaller and medium-sized farms are sought by agricultural workers on their way up the ladder, and by the sons of farmers who have been brought up in that profession. For the larger farms, there is competition as well from the successful business men who wish to combine urban employment with life in the country. The first groups are the more numerous and are likely to have the lowest earnings in alternative occupations; their calculations therefore are not based on the statistically average income in different trades.

Here again, it is mainly social characteristics which influence the proportion of a population that wishes to farm—the natural increase or decrease in the rural population, the ease of transfer between rural and urban occupations, the opportunities for obtaining education, the comparative standards of public services in town and country. If the population is fairly homogeneous and moves easily between occupations and between regions, the supply of farmers is not likely to exceed that level for which the average income is roughly equivalent to that obtainable in comparable situations elsewhere. But if the rural population is unable or unwilling to seek employment outside agriculture, if it is increasing rapidly in numbers, then the pressure to obtain occupation of any piece of land may be so great that rural incomes remain relatively low. For this pressure will show itself either in high and rising values for land to be bought, which means that many who would farm cannot find the purchase price and remain landless workers; or in high rents and lower incomes from land available on lease; or in the small area of land available for each family which results from continuous subdivision among equal heirs.

The contrast between the wealthy industrialised countries and those still largely dependent on primitive agriculture shows most clearly in the divergent policies adopted to meet the demand for farms. If the alternative to life on an inadequate patch of land is the risk of unemployment and starvation in a town, national welfare is not improved by consolidating farms into larger units and throwing substantial numbers of families out to starve, even though such a policy might lead to better farming. Labour which cannot be employed elsewhere has no exchange value—no 'opportunity cost'; therefore, in an over-crowded economy, it can be applied intensively to land to a degree which would be quite uneconomic if it were costed at commercial rates. Where land and capital are both scarce and dear, output is forced by the excessive application of labour, sometimes to the point where there is no physical gain from the extra people employed. But since this surplus population exists, official policy can only attempt to regulate the terms on which land is available, by controlling rents, by putting a maximum to the size of farm, by compelling the re-distribution of the surplus to landless families. The break-up of large farms into small units and the transfer of ownership to the occupiers has recently been carried out both in Egypt and India, countries where the rise in population has created situations of this type.[1]

The objective of this policy may, not unfairly, be described as 'the equalisation of misery'; where poverty is general and

[1] D. Warriner, *Land Reform and Development in the Middle East*, ch. 1, R.I.I.A., 1957; M. Srinivasan, *Indian Journal of Agricultural Economics*, vol. xii, No. 2 (1957), p. 110.

for the present inescapable, social equity requires that as many families as possible should have a minimum area of land without paying an exorbitant rent to a small number of landowners, or an exorbitant interest to a small number of moneylenders. But such reforms in ownership and in farm sizes have at times led to a retrogression in farming techniques and to a falling off in the supply of produce to the towns, since it was usually the most efficient men who managed the large farms whence came most of the surplus over local consumption. Experience has shown that a policy of sub-division urgently needs to be combined with measures to promote better farming on the small units—basic education in simple improvements, the consolidation of scattered holdings, the supply of capital for fertilisers, drainage or irrigation, the promotion of co-operative societies for marketing, the purchase of supplies, or for the operation of costly implements.

Any community whose wealth is mainly derived from agriculture and whose population is increasing may find itself, to a greater or lesser extent, faced with a conflict between technical efficiency, which may require a larger average size of farms, and equality of opportunity, which implies the subdivision of farms into smaller and more numerous units. Arguments over these two objects have been going on in Britain since the agricultural revolution of the late eighteenth and early nineteenth centuries. The changes which took place at that time tended generally to a fall in the number of part-time holdings, often associated with grazing rights on common pasture; such holdings contributed little to the agricultural output but did provide a minimum of subsistence to families otherwise dependent on wages, and also a ladder by which some wage earners could climb to the rank of farmer. In that period of war, rising population and rapid industrial development, public opinion as expressed in Parliament favoured the consolidation of farms and the extinction of common grazing rights; these were regarded as essential steps towards a greater output, the urgent need for which over-rode other considerations. But towards the end of the nineteenth century, there was a marked change of sentiment which led to the provision of small-holdings by County Councils and other organisations, created by the purchase and breaking up of larger farms. The Small-Holdings Acts of 1892 and later years reflected partly the unsatisfied demand from agricultural workers and farmers' sons in many areas for small farms to be rented; and partly the half-nostalgic wish of reformers and social workers to re-create a vanished peasantry.

But the process of industrialisation, the increasing material wealth which results and the public provision of many social amenities in the towns has gradually made such a policy impossible. As was noted earlier, many of these small farms cannot, even with improved techniques, provide a minimum income judged appropriate to current standards. Yet there is a natural stickiness which keeps a race of farmers pinching, grumbling but still farming on inadequate areas, even though alternative jobs are available at higher incomes in other occupations. The appropriate policy for a Government aiming at economic efficiency is to encourage the outflow from farming and the amalgamation of farms by all methods short of provoking an intolerable political uproar. Such amalgamations have been proceeding naturally in many upland areas ever since the depression at the end of the nineteenth century, as in mid-Wales, one of the problem areas recently investigated. Since 1958, grants have been available to improve the capital equipment of small farms that can economically support a family, with the unwritten hope that those too small to be eligible will gradually disappear.[1] In Sweden, since the second world war, the State has scheduled certain holdings as uneconomic, so that, when they fall vacant, they cannot be transferred or sold in the open market, but have to be combined with others in the vicinity.[2] In the more fluid society of the United States, a similar process has resulted in the last two decades by the voluntary outflow of farming families seeking higher incomes in other occupations, as was shown in Table 17. For in urbanised and industrialised societies, equality of opportunity does not depend on access to land; it depends far more on access

[1] Agricultural Land Commission, *Report on Mid-Wales* (Cmd. 9631, 1955 and Cmd. 9809, 1956); *Assistance for Small Farmers* (Cmnd. 553, 1958).

[2] F. Meissner, 'Agrarian Reform in Sweden', *J.A.E.*, vol. XI, No. 4 (1956), pp. 444–56.

to education and freedom to move between occupations, between regions and between social groups.

III. THE EFFICIENCY OF MANAGEMENT

On most farms the farmer supplies simultaneously the capital, much of the labour and all the decisions, from choosing the farm to choosing the speed at which the tractor shall work. The profits of the farm depend primarily on his skill in judging what to produce, how much to produce of each commodity and what combination of resources gives the lowest possible cost. Each farmer has a framework of fixed factors which limits his choice in these decisions. Technical conditions may restrict his choice of crops; he may not be able to add to his farm, nor easily alter its lay-out; he may be short of capital; his supply of labour may be limited to the members of his family or by the scarcity of housing. The profitable employment of any one factor may depend on the supply of other complementary factors in proportions often dictated by technology but some-times variable within limits. Up to a point, therefore, capital in the form of machinery can be a substitute for labour; capital and labour can substitute for land by using the store stock or the feeding stuffs grown on other farms; crop spraying on contract may save costly labour and equipment used in cultivations. Modern technology has enormously increased the possible combinations of input which farmers have to consider in their search for the lowest possible costs; and by so doing has probably increased the difficulties of efficient management.

In any community at a given stage of development, farmers are likely to find their planning dominated by the scarcity and dearness of one particular factor, whether land, or labour, or machinery or capital or seasonal credit. Successful manage-ment then depends on applying the most profitable combination of other factors to that which is most scarce. Consider, for instance, the relative costs of land and labour indicated by the farm budget given by Professor Bradley, Professor of Botany in the University of Cambridge, for an eastern counties arable farm about 1720, with the similar type of farm about 1956. Professor Bradley calculated that 300 acres of arable land worked on a rotation of two grain crops and a fallow would cost £150 in rent; that the annual labour bill would average £30–£40 a year; that the equipment of the farm would cost some £450; and that gross receipts should be approximately the same sum. In 1956 a group of arable farms in North Essex, averaging 210 acres in size, spent on the average £440 in rent, £1,686 on labour, £1,754 on machinery, and carried tenants' capital valued at nearly £10,000 apiece, with gross receipts of much the same size.[1] It would not be at all surprising to find that a farmer was operating in 1956 precisely the same farm equipped with the same buildings, only somewhat modified, as that farmed by Professor Bradley's young man of 1720.[1]

Where land is dear because it is scarce, and labour cheap because it is plentiful, the most profitable combination of factors is likely to be one with much labour on a small area of land; profits will be highly correlated with output per acre. Where labour is dear and scarce, and land is cheap and easily come by, the successful farmer will adjust his acres and his cropping to obtain the best advantage from his labour; a high output per man will then be his compass to the most profitable combination of inputs. But many British farmers are operating today on farms whose size, lay-out and equipment grew piecemeal over the centuries; they each run a separate business which is small by the standards of modern industry and whose efficiency is further handicapped by the lumpiness of many inputs such as labour or the larger items of equipment. It is not therefore surprising that capital and labour is often used inefficiently in farming, in the sense that some of it could earn higher rewards in other trades. Mr J. O. Jones carried out a statistical analysis of the marginal value in relation to marginal cost of the use of land, labour and capital in a sample of farms[2]; he came to the tentative conclusions that about 35 per cent of the dairy farms, 12 per cent of the crop farms and 15 per cent of the mixed farms were 'overmanned', employing more labour than the cost warranted; but even higher proportions were

[1] R. Bradley, *The Complete Body of Husbandry, 1727;* Dept. of Agriculture, Farm Economics Branch, Cambridge, Report, No. 46 (1957).

[2] J. O. Jones, 'The Productivity of Major Factors in British Farming', *Farm Economist* (1956), No. 4, pp. 1–20; No. 5, pp. 11–20.

undermanned and could profitably have used more labour at the current price, if it had been available. These results arise either because labour is discontinuous and cannot be divided into small units to suit the small farms; or because much of it is family labour which is not, therefore, costed in the normal way; or because farmers have not accurately adjusted their various inputs to the prevailing levels of costs and returns. Indeed, it is difficult to see how farmers can achieve the theoretically perfect combination of factors in times of rapid technological change and rapidly changing prices, not only for their products but also for their inputs. But it is not difficult to see why, in farming, a considerable amount of these factors, common to all economic activity, can only earn a monetary reward less than could be obtained in other occupations.

Further Reading

A. W. Menzies-Kitchin, *Labour Use in Agriculture*, Department of Agriculture, Farm Economics Branch, Cambridge, Report No. 36 (1951).

F. G. Sturrock and D. B. Wallace, *The Family Farm*, Department of Agriculture, Farm Economics Branch, Cambridge. Occasional Papers No. 4 (1956).

H. T. Williams, 'Changes in the Productivity of Labour in British Agriculture', *J.A.E.* vol. x, No. 4 (1954), pp. 332–55.

G. P. Hirsch, 'Migration from the Land in England and Wales', *Farm Economist*, vol. vi, No. 9 (1951), pp. 270–80.

'Labour on the Land in England and Wales', *Farm Economist*, vol. viii, No. 2 (1955), pp. 13–23.

E. O. Heady, *Economics of Agricultural Production and Resource Use* (New York, 1952).

F. G. Sturrock, *Farm Accounting and Management*. 3rd edition (1957).

CHAPTER VIII

CONCLUSIONS

Even the highly simplified account contained in the preceding chapters must have shown how complex is the structure of agriculture and how intricate the mesh of long-term economic trends with short-term influences. Those who make agricultural policies, and those who have to work under them, need to bear in mind the conflicting nature of differing objectives; and while immersed in the problems of today, they must discern the economic forces which are invisibly shaping tomorrow.

I. CONFLICTS IN OBJECTIVES

In some countries today the urgent need is the largest and swiftest increase in food production, in order to feed not only an increasing number of people but also to secure a better diet for most of them. The urgent need for more food may bring about a substantial rise in the prices obtained for it, a rise which represents a transference of real income from the urbanised buyers to the agricultural sellers and also the mechanism which enables the sellers to expand their investment and extend their output. But a Government which depends more on the urban electorate than on rural support may find itself committed to 'keeping down the cost of living' by a policy of price control or State purchase at stable prices, even though such measures may discourage the production of more food; and within farming itself, those who would naturally lead in agricultural progress may be held back by limits on farm sizes or by high taxation. In such ways the objective of less inequality in income clashes with the objective of greater output.

At the other extreme, agricultural output may increase so rapidly, under the influence of technical innovations, that agricultural prices fall relatively to industrial prices, and farm incomes fall substantially below those obtained in comparable occupations. In such circumstances, the most economic use of resources dictates the transference of numbers of farm families into urban areas and industrial jobs, and the transference of some marginal land into, perhaps, national parks. But the fall in incomes required to effect these changes may be so severe and so widespread as to cause not only grave hardship but serious political unrest. A Government may then be pushed into schemes for maintaining prices in the interest of the marginal groups and may accumulate large stocks of unsaleable farm products representing the use of resources some of which could have produced other and more valuable commodities. The plea for stability in farm incomes then conflicts with the more general object of securing the highest value of output from the existing resources of land and capital and labour. The economist cannot decide for his nation the relative values to be attached to these various objectives—more food, greater equality of incomes, the maximisation of the current national income, political stability. But he should at least be able to diagnose the existence of such conflicts between incompatible objectives and to foresee the probable effects of proposed measures on both the immediate problems and on the long-term trends in economic affairs.

II. TRENDS AND DECISIONS

One of the most difficult aspects of policy making is precisely this distinction between the enduring forces which shape the basic economic structure and the temporary eddies on the surface. Yet such a distinction is of the utmost importance. If the policy makers change their plans with every passing wave, their actions may be nullified by the flow of the tide beneath the surface and they will be in danger of aimless drifting. Yet if they pay no attention to the waves, if they entirely ignore current problems, the policy makers may be swept out of office by a temporary but overwhelming disturbance. Again, these long-term trends are themselves not unchanging; it is not easy to discern from the surface phenomena when the tide has altered and a new policy is required.

In recent years, applied economists have developed a number of tools for measuring these long-term trends. The growth of the national income and of output per head, the level of investment in various types of resource, variations in the terms of trade between farm and industrial products, the relation between family income and demand for food at different income levels—these theoretical concepts are now being measured more or less accurately in contemporary societies; for a few countries, these basic trends have been analysed for the past hundred years or even for a longer period. As a result we now have a better understanding of the forces which determined the character of recent decades. At the same time, there have been prolonged studies of the short fluctuations in industrial and agricultural prosperity—the trade cycle in general, the ups and downs of agricultural prices, the changes between farm incomes, farm outputs and farm inputs. Valuable as all this analysis has been, the policy makers still have to distinguish, year by year, between the permanent and the temporary, to decide whether to project current trends into the future as a guide to action, or to assume a reversal of some important trend. The modern nation is an incredibly complex organisation; no planning authority can fully know, or accurately foresee, what may happen in every part, let alone predict the influences that may impinge from international markets and from other Governments. Yet incomplete knowledge, imperfect analysis and inadequate administration will none of them absolve a Government in the twentieth century from the necessity of having an agricultural policy of some kind or another. And whatever agricultural policy is chosen must be based, firstly, on the existing economic structure and, secondly, on the existing trends in development so far as they can be ascertained.

III. MECHANISMS OF POLICY

I. LAISSER-FAIRE

A Government may decide that agricultural planning may be left to the operation of a market system, within the general framework of laws, customs and social structure. Its policy is then to allow each of its citizens, within this framework, to act and move freely as each of them thinks will best suit his own interest. State action may then be limited to the collection of statistics, the publication of market reports, the control of infectious diseases among animals and plants, the provision of scientific research and of education in agricultural techniques; it may possibly organise also a farm advisory service in order to make the results of research quickly available to farmers.

Given a fully commercialised economy, the agricultural structure that results will reflect the individual plans of thousands of farmers, farm workers and suppliers of farm services. Planning will be decentralised and initiative allowed full play on all these thousands of units, within the limits set by their individual rigidities and by the risks and uncertainties they each face. There may be no general pre-conceived plan but there will emerge a clearly defined pattern of agricultural output, agricultural incomes and farm structure, adapted to the main trends in prices and costs and techniques.

This type of planning can reasonably be combined with specific measures designed to make market influences more effective or to protect those whose bargaining power is unduly weak. If processors of a staple food are few in number and operate on a large scale, then market prices may reflect not so much the long-term changes in demand and supply as the growth of monopolistic power. In such cases, a policy of laisser-faire might, not illogically, be combined with a policy of 'trust-busting' on the American model; or competitors might be encouraged to enter the trade; or the State itself might regulate the prices offered to producers. Again, it may be found that the lack of 'market intelligence' among scattered agricultural workers has created wide disparities in wages between different districts. Some compulsory organisation for negotiating and enforcing minimum wages may then usefully help to equalise the bargaining power between farmers and farm workers in thousands of individual wage agreements.

It is also not illogical for the State to assume responsibility for activities which cannot be brought within a market economy to an adequate degree. Individuals working within the framework of one life-time may under-estimate the value to the economy as a whole of such investment as afforestation or soil conservancy; if the State does not promote such policies, they may not be carried out at all. These activities are also likely to require investment in such large units, spread over such a length of time, that individuals cannot assume the risk without the backing of a well-organised administration on a national scale, which can, if necessary, apply compulsion to individual citizens. And particularly where land is concerned, actions planned by individuals can, in total, defeat the intention behind those actions. If one farmer drains his land so as to discharge on to his neighbour's, there is no gain in national welfare; if half a million citizens decide to move out of the metropolis and live in the country round it, travelling up and down each day, they merely create suburbia, destroy the country and fail to achieve what they wished as individuals. These individual actions or investments may most nearly bring about what was intended if some controlling authority supervises the schemes of drainage, prevents building on parks and playing fields near towns, and regulates the balance between detached houses and vertical flats. When an individual uses land for a purpose which yields him the best economic return, his action may incidentally subtract from the economic return obtained from adjacent land; the total gain from a number of such actions is therefore far less than is expected, unless the individuals concerned are made to take into account the indirect loss which results from their separate plans.

2. CONTROL THROUGH PUBLIC FINANCE

At a second stage, a Government may maintain a general control over the development of the national economy, through financial measures applied alike to agriculture and to industry. The maintenance of full employment by judicious regulation of investment, protection of the balance of payments by exchange controls, the imposition of taxes to check expenditure or sudden inflation, the redistribution of incomes over time (as by children's allowances or compulsory pensions) or between social groups—such measures are now part of the general armament of most Governments in their perpetual battle against the trade cycle, against the destitution of individuals or general exchange crises. Within this framework of general control, the planning of each economic unit may be left, as before, to the influence of market prices operating through the decisions of its operator. In making those decisions, he will be influenced by the price he has to pay for borrowed capital, by supplies of imported machinery, by purchase tax on other requirements or by the imposition of income tax on his own earnings. The Government will have a general economic policy but not specifically an agricultural one.

From the middle of the nineteenth century, the agriculture of the United Kingdom functioned under the first of these two policies. The second gradually became more prominent, as Government began to take a wider view of its functions and to assume greater responsibility for the general progress of the community and for the distribution of incomes within it. But Britain was the exception in having for nearly a century no other specifically agricultural policy than that imposed by a free market, open to all the influences of international trade. In most European countries in modern times, and in the United Kingdom after 1932, Governments have adopted tariffs or import controls in order to mitigate the impact of such external trade on the internal level of agricultural prices, incomes and production.

3. IMPORT CONTROLS

The analysis of the previous chapters has indicated three important characteristics of agriculture in modern societies. These are, firstly, the instability of some prices under the impact of a small surplus of supplies; secondly, the increase in supplies of most agricultural products; and thirdly, the tendency for agricultural incomes generally to fall below earnings in other and comparable occupations. These last trends have become most marked over the past fifty years, when the reduction in transport costs, the continuous improvement in methods of food preservation and the practical application of science have combined to unify to a marked degree the various local and regional markets for the staple agricultural products. Over a long period, these trends, if allowed their full influence, would have provided food buyers with more regular and possibly larger supplies at lower prices, but in each market there would be groups of producers who would have been forced through a long period of financial distress before they either quitted agriculture or developed some new type of farming. Further, the smooth flow of international trade has been so broken by wars, exchange crises and periodic devaluations over the past thirty years that the benefits of such specialised production appeared uncertain, and its disadvantages dangerous to national security. Consequently, practically all Governments have adopted various types of import controls in order to insulate to some extent their national pattern of agriculture from the immediate impact of external prices. Since such measures have become so general, an analysis of their general effects is an important part of agricultural economics; but the reader is warned that what follows in this section is a highly simplified account of an exceptionally intricate part of economic theory. The effect of tariffs and import controls is related to the supply and demand in the individual markets concerned, to the general level of prices in the countries exchanging goods, and to the market for international payments, by which the currency of one nation can be converted into those of all others with whom it has trading relations. Here we can only deal with the principal points as they relate to the markets in agricultural products.

The normal effect of imposing a moderate tariff, or of raising the rate of duty, is to reduce the volume of imports and thus to raise internal prices. How much imports will be reduced by any given duty depends on the elasticity of supply from foreign countries. If there is no alternative market for the product concerned, and the producers have little prospect of making equal profits from other types of production, then the main effect of an import duty may be to lower the returns to the foreign suppliers and there will be little effect on the volume of supplies or on the price. Again, if demand is highly elastic to a rise in price, a reduction in foreign supplies may cause only a small rise in price, since demand falls off almost equally. In the first case, the importing country gains by the amount collected in duty, but in the second its consumers lose a substantial amount of satisfaction. Because the rise in prices in either case is small, there is little scope for increased production in the home country, unless here, too, supply is exceptionally elastic. Again, if the imported product is becoming progressively cheaper because of falling transport costs, the effect of an import duty will be measured not by a rise in price or reduction in supplies, but by the difference between the stable home price and the falling price in external markets, by the volume of imports which would have occurred in the absence of such duty. It is therefore very difficult to estimate the effect of import duties, or even of import quotas, without a careful study of the conditions of supply and demand for the commodity concerned, with all the complexities of changing techniques or perhaps of seasonal fluctuations in supply or demand. But we may be able to analyse the results of such an action if we consider (a) whether the change which we wish to eliminate or reduce is likely to be permanent or temporary; and (b) what alternative use could be made of the factors of production likely to be rendered redundant if imports are attracted by a free market.

Let us consider the severe fall in cereal prices which took place in the last quarter of the nineteenth century. This was the result mainly of the fall in transport costs by land and sea which enabled grain to be profitably grown in the central states of North America and sold in Europe. The falling prices brought immediately a fall in the price of the basic foodstuff of the urban population in countries open to the increased supply. There may have been some increase in wheat consumption among the poorest, but most consumers found themselves with money in hand, after they had bought all the bread they wanted; they spent that money on a variety of goods, including more meat, dairy products, eggs and other foods. The same fall in cereal prices drastically reduced the incomes of those farmers producing cereals in Europe and in the eastern side of the United States and eventually the capital values or the rents of their farms. Many, though not all, of these now high-cost wheat growers were able to turn their resources to the production of the foods for which there was now a growing demand, and in this they were assisted by the falling costs of cereal feeds. Those farmers tied to cereal production by physical conditions were compelled to reduce their costs through better management, improved practices or rapid mechanisation. In Britain, the area of wheat fell by more than 1½ million acres between 1875 and 1895 but even at the new and relatively lower prices, there were still nearly 1½ million acres under wheat at the later date. Improved diets at lower costs, a rising standard of life for the expanding population, a low-cost agriculture based more on livestock and less on cereals—these were achieved at the cost of financial loss and hardship, sometimes severe, to a number of farmers, landowners and farm workers. But most of the resources formerly used in cereal growing found employment, either in some other type of agricultural production or in occupations other than agriculture; there does not appear to have been any appreciable quantity of derelict arable land in Britain over this period.

In Denmark, another free-trade country, this shift in the relative level of cereal and livestock prices stimulated the export trade in meat and dairy produce, mainly to Britain and the industrial countries of western Europe. Using home-grown and imported cereals, Danish farmers secured a rising real income for themselves and their country, in which agriculture remained for many decades the principal employment. At the same time, the farmers in the new wheat lands beyond the sea, and all transport trades benefited by the opening up of these new markets. The international specialisation in production which followed from the comparative advantages of wheat-growing in North America led thus to an increase in real income for almost everyone except those high-cost farmers, their farm workers and rent-receivers whose incomes took the first impact of the change.

But other countries in western Europe shielded their agriculture from these falling cereal prices by imposing import duties; their rural communities did not, therefore, have to undergo at that time the same drastic social and economic changes. But equally, neither did the buyers of their grain benefit from the increase in real income which might have followed from lower prices. In most of these countries, agriculture was still the largest single occupation; the political influence of farmers or of landowners was strong, while that of the urban food buyers was relatively weak; and though industry was expanding, it was not certain that all those who might be displaced from cereal production would necessarily and immediately find alternative jobs. Further, it was considered militarily dangerous to depend unduly upon foreign supplies for a basic foodstuff. For all these reasons it was thought desirable to preserve the existing relationship between incomes of different groups of farmers and the existing structure of agriculture. In short, the principal objective was stability, but stability in the face of a change in relative prices which was to prove durable and conspicuous.

If markets were free of all controls, the level of profitable output from British agriculture would be set by the international price level for agricultural products, operating against the level of costs in the British markets for the labour and other requisites which farmers buy. And this price-level would indirectly control the level of profits obtained from the production even of commodities without competing imports, such as liquid milk, since the pattern of mixed farming common in Britain can usually be adjusted fairly easily to produce rather more of one and rather less of another product, in accordance with relative profitability. The periods when prices of agricultural products were rising against the prices of manufactured goods—the middle decades of the nineteenth century, the years immediately after the first and second world wars—were therefore periods when farming profits rose, and British farm production tended to expand, both absolutely and in its share of total food supplies. Conversely, when agricultural prices were falling on international markets, the volume of food imports tended to increase, thus bringing down British prices to the level of those elsewhere, as occurred after 1875, again between the wars and since 1953.

Now it is quite natural for farmers and market-gardeners, confronted with a rising volume of imports and a falling level of prices and of profits, to seek to exclude the first in order to prevent the second. But a nation which has barely 6 per cent of its population engaged in agriculture clearly cannot make itself better off by raising the price of food bought by the other 94 per cent. If, by tariffs and quotas, British consumers pay 6s. per dozen for eggs some of which could be imported for

5s. per dozen, then consumers will buy fewer eggs than they otherwise would; resources of capital and labour are being devoted to producing eggs to sell at 6s. per dozen which might add more to the national output if they were used in some other industry in which Britain has a relative advantage over other countries. Further, a rise in food prices, absolute or relative to those elsewhere may lead to an offsetting rise in money wages; if that occurs, there will be a general rise in internal costs which will again reduce the profits not only of farmers but also of the exporting industries.

Such arguments dominated the national policy in the last quarter of the nineteenth century and again in the decade after the first world war. But in the nineteen-thirties normal price relationships were swept aside by peculiarly violent fluctuations in demand and supply, which brought severe and long-continued unemployment in most countries. Moderate measures of import control were adopted by Britain after 1931 as a defence against these temporary disturbances. The import duties chiefly affected fresh fruit and vegetables, meat, processed milks and manufactured foods, but were applied only to imports from foreign countries. Their effects on total supplies or on internal prices were therefore doubtful, but they possibly raised some prices and undoubtedly caused some diversion in supplies in favour of Commonwealth growers. The quota on bacon imports definitely raised the prices of Danish bacon by reducing its supply rather faster than the output of British bacon rose, while the price of the latter rose more slowly; there was a wider margin between the two, showing that many housewives preferred the dearer Danish product because of its uniform high quality, to the variable and unfamiliar British bacon. Almost all food-importing countries adopted in these years import controls far more rigid and severe than those imposed by the British Government, in order, similarly, to protect the existing pattern of incomes and production. Such protective measures were carried through the second world war to operate again in the troubled post-war years. For war once again disorganised international markets and exchange rates and stimulated wide variations between the agricultural prices ruling in different countries.

CONCLUSIONS

For five years of war and for five years afterwards, British agricultural policy was dominated by food shortages, induced first by the scarcity of shipping, then by the scarcity of grain in world markets and finally by the scarcity of foreign exchange with which to buy imports. British agriculture was greatly expanded under a system of fixed prices designed to induce the maximum output of a few basic foods—grain, potatoes, milk and latterly pigmeat—almost irrespective of costs. This distorted structure had gradually to be re-adapted to the new pattern of international trade as it revived from 1948 onwards, with a new pattern of agricultural prices considerably higher than before the war in relation to prices for manufactured goods. The terms of trade, that is, had become less favourable to Britain, an exporter of manufactured goods and a large importer of foods and raw materials. In the decade before 1939, one unit of manufactured goods could buy on world markets one-quarter to one-third more agricultural products than in

Table 21. *Terms of trade on world markets*

1913	100	1947–49	98
1923–26	90	1950–51	118
1927–30	85	1952–53	105
1931–34	64	1954–55	106
1935–38	72		

* Prices on world markets of agricultural products compared
with prices of manufactured goods.

Source: F.A.O., *State of Food and Agriculture, 1956*, p. 65.

1913 (Table 21), but after 1947 the ratio fell sharply to one-fifth less in 1950–51 than in 1913. This trend implied that the same volume of imports would cost more in terms of exports; and that, in order to equalise costs at the margin between home and foreign produce, it would be advisable to produce at home a higher proportion of total food supplies than before the war, though a lower proportion than in the years of food shortages. It was of course impossible to foresee how long these relatively unfavourable terms of trade would last and in fact agricultural prices have been falling fairly steadily (relative to manufacturing prices) from the peak reached during the Korean war.

Under the Agriculture Act, 1947, successive Governments

continued the war-time system of fixed prices for the products of British farms, but after 1952 these were gradually replaced by a more flexible system of 'deficiency payments', designed to repay to producers any deficiency between current market prices and standard prices. The current market prices reflect the factors of internal demand and of supply, both from British and overseas farmers; the standard prices, those received by British farmers, have generally followed the trend in market prices but at a much slower pace; they have been above market prices for most commodities for most of the period since de-control. In addition to these deficiency payments, which are described in more detail below, there have been moderate import duties on a number of products—bacon, beef and veal, and many fruits and vegetables. (There are also import duties on many things which farmers buy, such as machinery, oilseeds from foreign countries, etc.).

The prices received by British farmers have therefore generally been higher than those on international markets, but not necessarily higher than those paid to overseas producers in their domestic markets. For other countries have followed a similar policy by different means, so that large discrepancies exist between producer prices in different countries, even when they trade fairly freely. Table 22 shows the variation in wheat prices ruling in Europe and North America in 1955/6 as a result of price controls of all types. The long-term disadvantages of such measures derive from this separation of markets, perpetuating high-cost production when there are cheaper sources of supply. Yet these disadvantages are commonly regarded as outweighed by the partial insulation to national agricultures, based on a wide variety of soils, climates and past structures, against trends which would level out regional variations in price and concentrate certain types of production in areas of lowest costs.

There are two groups of countries whose agricultural prices are strongly influenced by international markets—the principal importers, of which the United Kingdom is the chief, and the principal exporters. Taking New Zealand as an example of the latter group, the exports of meat, dairy produce and wool account for more than 90 per cent of total exports; most of

Table 22. *Producer prices for wheat in various countries, 1955/6*

Country	Dollars per quintal	Remarks
Norway	12·60	Fixed price
Sweden	7·73	Fixed price
Denmark	6·76	Free price for 1954/5
United Kingdom	8·27	Guaranteed minimum price
Eire	7·72	Fixed price
Netherlands	6·69	Fixed price
Belgium	8·99	Target price
Luxembourg	10·59	Fixed price
France	8·45	Fixed price for 92 % of sales
Germany	10·01 ⎱ 10·37 ⎰	Fixed limits for prices by regions
Switzerland	13·53 ⎱ 15·64 ⎰	Fixed price varied by quality, extra for mountain wheat
Canada	4·54	Initial pooled price for No. 1 Northern
U.S.A.	7·65	Support price

Source: 'O.E.E.C. Agricultural Policies in Europe and North America' (May 1956), p. 366. Prices converted into dollars at exchange rates ruling in December 1955.

the meat and dairy produce has been sold to the United Kingdom and much of the wool is also sold through London. Price fluctuations on the British markets thus react directly on to the whole New Zealand economy. Nor can the non-agricultural sector subsidise farming to any extent, for agriculture is the largest single industry in the nation. The profits of New Zealand farmers and the volume of foreign exchange available generally for imports thus depend on successful competition in markets over which the New Zealand Government has little influence and which are subject to large fluctuations. During and since the war, the immediate impact of price changes has been cushioned by the operations of the marketing boards for meat, wool and dairy produce which accumulated substantial reserves from the high prices ruling at the end of the war and again in 1951/2; these reserves were drawn upon in the years of falling prices after 1955. But once these are exhausted, it will not be possible to prevent international prices from reacting directly on to incomes and costs, and through agriculture on to the national economy as a whole.

Agricultural policy in New Zealand is therefore concerned firstly with these averaging schemes operated by the Marketing Boards, and secondly with securing a high degree of efficiency in the basic types of farming, so that expansion can continue in sales to the competitive markets which they supply.

4. CONTROL OF COMMODITY PRICES

The purpose of import restrictions has been to maintain a level of prices (and therefore of incomes and of domestic production) different from that which would be brought about in free markets open to international influences. Usually, though not always, the international prices have been judged too low and import controls operate with supporting measures to keep up domestic prices. Unfortunately, prices influence other things as well as incomes. They also equate demand with immediately available supply and partly regulate the volume of supplies. The control of internal prices in order to give a desired level of income may therefore have surprising results on the flow of supplies, and on the rate at which those supplies can be sold. The administrators of prices usually find that their actions create acute problems elsewhere, and are thereby compelled to buttress their import control with price control, production control, sales control, purchase of unsold stocks and even the periodic destruction of an embarrassing surplus. These difficulties can be illustrated from the agricultural policy of two countries, the United States and the United Kingdom, both of which have rejected the price level provided by free markets for agricultural products.

The American legislation requires the Government to maintain, within limits, that relationship between the prices which farmers pay for their requisites and those which they receive which existed in the years before the first world war.[1] Whenever the prices of the controlled commodities fall below the required parity level by more than a certain proportion, the administration is required to accumulate stocks, thus taking supplies off the market, or to restrict supplies, after agreement with the producers concerned. The formula, it should be noted, relates

[1] O.E.E.C. 'Agricultural Policies in Europe and North America', July 1957. F.A.O., *The State of Food and Agriculture, 1958*, pp. 27–30, 53–56.

only to prices, and ignores changes in efficiency—that is, in the amount of output obtained per unit of input. The maintenance of price relationships which balanced supply and demand fifty years ago has produced since the second world war an almost continuous over-supply, thanks to the science and technology now available to American farmers. Stocks have accumulated on a gigantic scale; the acreage of basic crops has been restricted but the effect has been nullified by the continuous rise in yields per acre. The maintenance in this way of minimum prices for cereals and for cotton, to take two examples, has had far-reaching results. It has kept up the cost of live-stock products, such as meat, butter and cheese, for which feeding cereals are an important input; it has fossilised a pattern of production which has little relevance to modern needs; it has impeded the exports of these basic crops, except under special schemes of inter-Governmental aid for which low prices have been allowed by legislation; and it has put a heavy burden on the finances of the central Government. But it has maintained farm incomes at a higher level than would other-wise have occurred; and by so doing, investment has probably been stimulated in new machinery and improved technology which in turn has led to increased supplies.

It is easy to criticise this heroic attempt to prevent a re-currence of the depression of 1929 by preserving for all time the price relationships of 1910–14. But few countries can escape the charge of reviving price relationships from the past as a substitute for price relationships likely to be suitable for the near future. In the United Kingdom, a standard price of 10s. per cwt. was introduced for wheat in 1932 because this was approximately the market price in the year before the depres-sion. The quota on bacon imports was designed to limit supplies to the level of 1927–9, in the expectation of restoring the prices of that year.

The Agriculture Act, 1947, made possible in the United Kingdom a more flexible method of maintaining a minimum level of agricultural income. Guaranteed minimum prices for the basic agricultural products are fixed by the Government as part of the annual review of agricultural output, costs, supplies and income and they operate through deficiency payments made whenever market prices are lower than those guaranteed. For cereals, the deficiency payments are made annually (or at shorter intervals for wheat) on the difference between the two prices on all sales by registered growers or on the area grown. The deficiency payments for fatstock relate market prices to seasonally adjusted minimum prices for a month at a time; for pigs and eggs, the guaranteed prices are also linked to the cost of a standard ration of feedingstuffs. The guaranteed price for sugar-beet, and for cane-sugar bought under Commonwealth agreements, is paid from a levy collected by the Sugar Board on all refined sugar produced or imported in the United Kingdom. For milk, eggs, potatoes and wool, the deficiency payments are made through Marketing Boards set up by producers under the Agricultural Marketing Acts, 1931–49, each operating under a different form of agreement with the Ministry of Agriculture.

Some of these Marketing Boards also exercise varying degrees of control over the volume of home supplies, and therefore over the prices received in the markets. The Potato Marketing Board varies with the yield the minimum size of potato that can be sold and thus keeps off the market a higher proportion of a larger crop; it also controls the area planted above the basic quotas which relate to the acreage grown in 1951–53. In addition, it buys potatoes surplus to the market at the approved price and re-sells them at much lower prices for stock feed or for processing; the loss is covered either from its own funds or from the deficiency payments. The Hops Marketing Board controls most strictly both the production and sale of hops, for which there is but one market—the brewers—and no guaranteed price. The Milk Marketing Boards receive guaranteed prices for all milk sold in the liquid market; as discriminating monopolists, they sell the surplus to manufacturers at the highest prices they can be induced to pay. Each producer then receives a pooled price, derived partly from the guarantees and partly from the manufacturers. The Wool Marketing Board sells all British fleece wool and operates an averaging scheme with the proceeds; farmers receive each year only the guaranteed price and any surplus obtained is put to reserve, to be drawn upon if market prices fall below the guaranteed price. Only when such reserves have been exhausted does the

Board draw from the State to maintain the guarantee. The Egg Marketing Board sells the output from the larger poultry farmers to the packing stations and receives a deficiency payment if the market price thus obtained is below that guaranteed, but a considerable though unknown volume of trade is conducted directly from producer to retailer or consumer outside these arrangements. None of these three Marketing Boards has as yet controlled output or sales of individual producers.

As market prices for the basic commodities have often been lower than those guaranteed, substantial payments have been required under the post-war policy, as shown by Table 23. It has been calculated that possibly two-thirds of these payments accrue to the two-thirds of the total output produced by the one-third of large farms which provide, even at market prices, substantial incomes to the efficient occupiers.[1] From one point of view, that is a desirable feature of a system which works by rewarding the efficient with larger incomes, and thus encouraging them to extend their businesses. From another point of view, the subsidies accentuate the inequality of incomes within farming created by the small size of so many units, which in turn restricts the efficiency of the occupiers. This latter opinion has so far prevailed in recent years that price subsidies have been increasingly supplemented by grants in aid of specific items of expenditure likely to be of special importance to small farms or to hill farms selling store stock for which there are no guaranteed prices. There have been grants for calf-rearing, for sheep and cattle on hill land, for drainage, fertilisers, water supplies, new buildings and fences and roads; and in 1959 special grants were allowed for general improvement schemes on small farms which could be made capable of supporting a farm family at acceptable standards.

However, this divorce of income from output creates three types of difficulties. The administration of these grants is complex and contentious since it involves distinctions between large and small, economic and non-economic where no such distinctions naturally occur. Secondly, the greater the flow of capital improvements, the greater ought to be the subsequent

[1] E. M. H. Lloyd, 'Some Thoughts on Agricultural Policy', *J.A.E.*, vol. XII, No. 2 (1957), pp. 128–42; *Assistance for Small Farmers* (Cmnd. 553, 1958).

Table 23. *Agricultural subsidies and grants in the United Kingdom, 1954/5 to 1957/8 (£m.)*

	1954/5	1955/6	1956/7	1957/8
Total sales of farm produce	1,311½	1,316½	1,382	1,560
Aggregate farm income	295	329	319½	354½
Commodity subsidies				
Cereals	12·6	35·9	26·0	51·2
Eggs..	20·0	16·0	33·7	45·8
Fatstock	50·2	52·3	74·7	82·6
Wool	—	—	0·2	1·5
Potatoes	—	—	0·5	6·7
Milk	32·8	34·5	21·3	12·9
Production grants	50·3	57·5	70·7	75·3

Source: E. H. Whetham *et alia, Record of Agricultural Policy, 1954–56; 1956-58;* Dept. of Agriculture, Farm Economics Branch, Cambridge, Occasional Papers Nos. 3, 5 (1957, 1958). *Annual Review and Determination of Guarantees* (Cmd. 9721, 1956, Cmnd. 109, 1957, Cmnd. 390, 1958, Cmnd. 696, 1959).

flow of produce on to the markets which may lower prices and incomes for all farmers taken together. And thirdly, by raising the current income of some farms, these grants may encourage some families to remain in agriculture who would otherwise have moved to other occupations where they could earn more.[1] (It may be noted that an attack was begun after the war on one cause of high costs and low incomes, the fragmentation of many farms; but the dairy farmers concerned, those in the parish of Yetminster in Dorset, rejected the improved lay-out, though grants were offered to meet some of the cost. The Government then abandoned further efforts at compulsory re-organisation of farm boundaries.)

In the United Kingdom, the effective guarantee of a certain level of aggregate agricultural income through deficiency payments and production grants has called forth a supply which, in conjunction with imports, can only be sold at prices lower than those guaranteed; this has been markedly so for milk, wheat, pigs and eggs. The general result is that British farmers obtain higher prices than other suppliers to the British market; British consumers have larger supplies at lower prices than they otherwise would; British taxpayers contribute between £200m. and £300m. annually to fill the gap; British agriculture

[1]See page 113 above.

Table 24. *Agricultural production in the United Kingdom, pre-war, 1944, 1954, 1958*

	Pre-war	1944	1954	1958
Million acres				
Grain	5·2	9·4	7·1	7·5
Potatoes	0·7	1·4	0·95	0·8
Temporary Grass	4·2	4·7	6·0	6·2
Permanent Grass	18·8	11·7	13·2	13·5
Million gallons	Pre-war	1944/5	1954/5	1958/9
Milk sold	1,563	1,594	2,138	2,252
Thousand tons				
Beef and veal	578	504	797	783
Mutton and lamb	195	140	182	200
Pigmeat	435	172	757	726
Eggs	385	177	552	695
Wool	34	27	34	36
Net output*	100	124	152	161

* Sales off farms and estimated production of units under one acre, less purchases of feeding-stuffs, seeds and store stock.
Source: Agricultural Statistics; for 1958/9, Cmnd. 696, 1958.

probably employs some resources which would earn more in some other use, but the stability in its aggregate earnings conduces, it is hoped, to greater efficiency in its operations. The pattern of output maintained by this system is more intensive than that which existed between the wars, producing more cereals and milk, employing fewer men but much more machinery and other inputs, such as fertilisers, buildings and technical advice (Table 24). Imports now provide a lower proportion of total supplies than between the wars. This trend has developed from the relatively unfavourable terms of trade which existed immediately after the war but its effects have been prolonged by the system of price guarantees in force under the Agriculture Act, 1947.

Almost all Governments have found themselves compelled in the modern world to attempt some control of some agricultural markets, for a variety of reasons. Rents have been controlled, usually in order to lower them and thus to raise the incomes of tenants relatively to those of landowners. The price of credit has been controlled, usually again in favour of the borrowing farmers. The markets for farm products have been controlled, sometimes to raise farmers' prices and therefore

Table 25. *U.K. output as percentage of total supplies in the U.K. of certain foods, pre-war and 1955*

	Percentage of total supplies	
	Pre-war	1955
Flour	12	24
Potatoes	94	92
Sugar	16	26
Beef		66
Mutton and lamb	49	32
Pork		91
Bacon and ham	34	44
Milk (all forms)	97	97
Butter	9	5
Cheese	24	33
Eggs and products	63	80

Sources: R. J. Hammond, *Food*. Vol. 1: 'The Growth of Policy' (H.M.S.O. and Longmans, 1951), adapted from Table V, p. 394; E. A. G. Robinson, *Agriculture in the British Economy* (I.C.I., 1957), p. 12.

their incomes; sometimes to mitigate fluctuations; sometimes to keep down retail prices and thus benefit consumers; sometimes to keep down the prices received by farmers for the benefit of Government revenue. Table 22 showed for one commodity, wheat, how diverse were the measures used and the domestic prices which resulted in a number of countries; Table 26 shows how widespread is the practice of market control for farm products.[1]

It is thus rare in the modern world for farmers to receive for their output free prices from uncontrolled markets. Either producer prices are divorced from market prices by a network of subsidies or taxes; or market prices are modified by administrative measures restricting supply or the number of buyers and sellers. Most farmers in these countries operate in 'a mixed economy' in which price trends created by changes in supply and demand are more or less modified with the aim of securing a different pattern of domestic output, or more stable farm incomes, or a different distribution of incomes within national communities.

[1] I have omitted from this discussion the various international schemes for price control for agricultural products; the reader is referred to the list at the end of this chapter for reading on this topic.

Table 26. *Control over domestic markets for agricultural products*

	Percentage of output with	
	direct controls	direct price fixing
Norway	90	50
Sweden	94	*
Denmark	80	2
United Kingdom	85	80
Eire	43	22
Netherlands	79	34
Belgium	39	35
France	72	30
Germany	75	22
Canada	60	25
U.S.A.	50	48

* None, unless prices fluctuate outside certain limits.

Source: 'O.E.E.C. Agricultural Policies in Europe and North America', adapted from Annexe, Table I, July 1957.

5. CONTROL OF FARM WAGES

Many countries have in the past attempted to control (usually in order to lower) the price of land as expressed in the rents paid by tenants to owners. The problems which induce such controls, and the problems which these controls in turn create, were briefly discussed in Chapter VI (p. 95). Here we may look at one other type of price control, that over agricultural wages, usually imposed in order to raise them.

In most industrialised countries over the past sixty or seventy years, farm workers have earned less for longer hours than the majority of industrial workers. This inequality of earnings has provoked a wide variety of administrative measures, ranging from legally enforced minimum wages to the provision of free advice on alternative employments. The more drastic the proposed remedy, the more important it becomes to understand the causes of the continuing disparity, and the immediate effects of any change in it.

In the first place, it is important to realise that, up to a point, the market for manpower behaves much like any other market. If the price obtained in farming is low, the primary reason is that supply to that occupation has been sufficiently large to meet demand at that price; if the supply was less, demand would have to be adjusted through a rising price. The excess supply which creates the disparity in wages may be due to a variety of causes: to inertia in the rural population; to the cost and risk of looking for employment elsewhere; to the existence of payments in kind or non-monetary benefits which outweigh the difference in cash; or to a shortage of houses. If the market price is raised, other things (including supply) remaining unchanged, then those employing labour will find that, at current levels of costs and output, some part of their expenditure on labour is not bringing in an equal value in gross output; and that a different combination of factors of production will lead to lower costs. Some farmers will thus buy less manpower; they may either reduce output or combine their fewer men with more machinery. There will be fewer jobs offering in agriculture; there will be men unemployed; there may be a smaller volume of total output from agriculture and a rise in food prices, especially for those products which use much labour—milk or vegetables or sugar-beet. In countries where unemployment is general and capital scarce, it is hardly possible to enforce a minimum wage higher than current levels without intensifying the lack of employment which is already the chief scourge of the landless worker. No benefit is conferred by making employment scarcer still, even if it were administratively possible to enforce a minimum wage on markets uncoordinated, widely dispersed and often confused by family relationships. Even in Britain between the wars, a minimum wage could hardly have been enforced at much above the market rate without causing unemployment in agriculture at a time when the numbers of industrial unemployed were never below one million.

But this argument against a minimum wage in general must be qualified in some situations. A minimum wage which can be enforced, either by trade unions or by legal measures, at about the current average rate can usefully level up disparities within agriculture created by the widely dispersed bargains between individual farmers and their men. By its nature, the market for farm labour is highly imperfect, since the commodity is not standardised and all sorts of non-monetary considerations enter into the bargain, from the temper of the farmer to the kind of house available. An unemployed worker in an over-stocked market may have little idea of the market rate, and cannot, without much suffering, refuse employment when offered it. A publically announced and legally enforced minimum may therefore level up the lowest wages offered. This levelling up of the lowest wages to the market average was perhaps the chief effect of the county Agricultural Wage Committees which operated in England and Wales from 1924, and in Scotland from 1938.

Secondly, a rise in wages may push the larger farmers who employ hired men into improving their management in general. A rise in wages may then lead to a marked rise in output per man and unemployment may be negligible; farmers may merely refrain from replacing workers as they leave, so that the decline in employment is gradual and the rise in costs not conspicuous. It is often argued, with much evidence, that a steady pressure to raise wages is the best inducement towards good management; and that such pressure has contributed towards that steady rise of some 2 to 3 per cent a year in the output per man which has become customary in British agriculture over the last twenty or thirty years. But clearly there are limits to this process. A rise in wages above this rate will cause a rise in costs, and unless prices are adjusted to suit, there will be a tendency both for farm output to be checked and for the number of farm jobs offered to fall. And if prices are adjusted upwards to cover the change in costs, then the buyers of agricultural produce face a rise in their costs which may set off a general claim for higher wages all round. The same result may occur by a more direct route if industrial workers react strongly to any change in customary differentials in wage rates. For nearly a century, the wages of farm workers in Britain have been substantially below the earnings of most other trades, and large groups of workers have come to associate their own skill and social standing as linked with a differential of so much above the farm rate. As noted on p. 109, every rise in the minimum wage for agriculture was apt to be followed by a rise in wages for trades closely connected —roadmen, lorry drivers, country railwaymen, builders' labourers, and before long the gap re-appeared. In post-war Britain, this process can be seen from Fig. 6, which also shows the relatively low earnings of the large number of men who operate the smallest farms. These holdings provide, on average, a cash income which is often below what the occupier could earn as a cowman on a larger farm; but they also provide the occupier with a business of his own and the social status of a

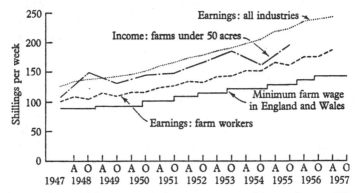

Fig. 6. Minimum agricultural wage, average weekly earnings and farm income in the United Kingdom, 1946-1958. (A = April, O = October), *Source:* See E. H. Whetham and J. I. Currie, *Record of Agricultural Policy,* Dept. of Agriculture, Farm Economics Branch, Cambridge (1958), Occasional Paper No. 5.

farmer who counts for more than a hired man in most rural communities. The stubborn existence of so many small farms is a pertinent reminder that money, with which the economist is principally concerned, is not the sole criterion by which human beings choose their life's work.

*   *   *   *

The last sections have described the recent agricultural policies of a number of countries which are fairly well industrialised. In these countries, agriculture has been transformed from a primitive occupation depending mainly on custom and tradition to a highly scientific and commercialised business, offering economic independence and a rural life to many thousands of families. It uses a wide range of industrial products and also competes in the national markets for its supplies of labour and capital. It has developed a persistent trend towards increased output on the one hand, and towards labour-saving devices on the other, as a reaction to the scarcity and rising wages of hired men. But this trend towards increased output is in constant danger of outrunning the capacity of national markets to consume extra quantities of basic foods, for which both price and income-elasticity is now low. Apart from periods of war or general restocking, the prices of most agricultural products thus have a long-term tendency to fall relatively to those of industrial products; and this trend in prices, which is required to equate demand with supply, produces a stable or falling level of aggregate income to agriculture as a whole, at a time when most other sections of these communities are enjoying a rise in their real income, partly because food is relatively cheap. This disparity in incomes has been mitigated by the fall in the number of persons employed in agriculture, but the family farms have proved to be remarkably stable units, even in the face of a considerable divergence in income levels. Hence in recent decades the agricultural policies of these countries have been designed largely to raise the average level of agricultural incomes, either by obstructing imports or by subsidising exports, by the regulation of internal prices or by many forms of special grants.

This transference of income has involved taxpayers and urban consumers in substantial costs. But the agricultural sector in these countries is relatively small; the mis-direction of resources which such policies may cause is slight relative to the total volume available for investment; and the cost has been paid out of industrial incomes which have themselves risen substantially in the last twenty-five or thirty years. Because of a nostalgic sentiment in favour of farm families, or because of memories of war-time food shortages, or because of political alignments, industrial populations seem willing, almost indefinitely, to support agricultural incomes and thus to retain in agricultural pursuits a number of families which contribute a lower value in output to the national pool of goods and services than they draw by income.

Such policies for the augmentation of agricultural incomes in industrialised economies have their origins in two trends—a demand for food which is rising only slowly because consumption is already high, and a supply, already large, which is increasing rapidly through the ready adoption of scientific knowledge and of technical innovations. But it is only rich countries that can afford to be extravagant in this way, and can allow agricultural incomes to be partly divorced from agricultural output. Similar policies may be highly dangerous for countries in which neither of these basic trends is operating, in which agriculture provides the largest part of the national output and the cost of food is the largest item in the national economy; for in such circumstances the misdirection of scarce resources may hinder more severely the needed rise in output. It may well be desirable for Governments to control or influence markets in order to mitigate fluctuations in prices and incomes and to protect those groups which are economically weak, but such actions are only likely to be beneficial if they work with, and not against, the current trends in market valuations.

Further Reading

O.E.E.C. Agricultural Policies in Europe and North America, 1956, 1957.
J. H. Kirk. 'Some Objectives of Agricultural Support Policy', *J.A.E.* vol. xiii, No. 2 (1958), pp. 134–51.
Economist Intelligence Unit, *Britain and Europe* (London, 1957), ch. IV.
Agriculture in the British Economy (I.C.I., London, 1957).
R. F. Harrod. *International Economics.* Cambridge Economic Handbook (1946).
E. H. Whetham *et alia, Record of Agricultural Policy, 1954–56; 1956–58;* Department of Agriculture, Farm Economics Branch, Cambridge, Occasional Papers Nos. 3, 5.
F.A.O., Commodity Policy Studies: *International Wheat Agreement* (1952); *Long Term Contracts* (1953); *International Sugar Agreement* (1953); *Agricultural Surpluses* (1954).

INDEX

Printed in the United States
By Bookmasters